HAUNTED LOUISIANA

Other Books in Pelican's
Haunted America Series

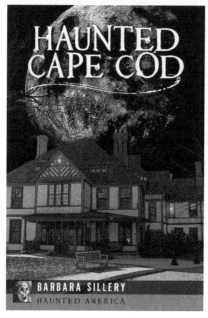

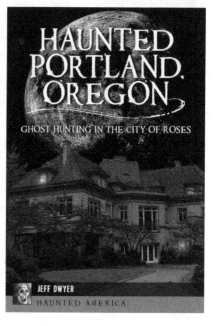

HAUNTED LOUISIANA

BARBARA SILLERY

PHOTOGRAPHS BY
OAK LEA AND DANIELLE GENTER

FOREWORD BY PHILLIP J. JONES

Haunted
America

PELICAN PUBLISHING
NEW ORLEANS 2022

The word "Pelican" and the depiction of a pelican are trademarks
of Arcadia Publishing Company Inc. and are registered
in the U.S. Patent and Trademark Office.

ISBN 9781455626649
Ebook ISBN 9781455626656

All photographs by Oak Lea unless otherwise indicated. Front-cover
photograph by Danielle Genter.

Published by Pelican Publishing
New Orleans, LA
www.pelicanpub.com

To my three muses:
Danielle Dawn
Rebecca Aimée
Heather ("Tinker Bell") Anne

Contents

Foreword

I am delighted to have appeared in Barbara Sillery's documentary, *The Haunting of Louisiana*. It was a pleasure to get to know Barbara, whose professional skill, enthusiasm, and charm were responsible for a delightful television program.

I am pleased that she has carried the project forward into a book, bringing to it all the talent she richly displayed in the earlier phase of this venture.

Louisiana's legacy from those who have gone before us is much greater than ghost tales. Louisiana is blessed with a culture and history that distinguish her from any other state. Her distinction is based on many elements, most of which stem from the various cultures that have so greatly influenced her character.

To those who may be encountering Louisiana for the first time through these wonderful stories—prepare to be engaged and entertained to a degree to which you are certainly unaccustomed. Part of your pleasure will come from the stories themselves and part from the style in which they are presented. Barbara's gift for storytelling holds in the written word just as it does before a television camera.

There is something in the dark, delta soil of Louisiana that leads some visitors to feel a compulsive tug at the sleeves—a signal to return. Small wonder, then, that there would be spirits unable to rest. They, like many of us, just can't imagine leaving Louisiana.

—Phillip J. Jones
Former Secretary, The Louisiana Department
of Culture, Recreation, and Tourism

Preface

In nature nothing dies.
From each sad remnant of decay,
Some forms of life arise.
—Charles Mackay

Ghost, spirit, bogeyman, loup garou, feu follet, pirate, voodoo queen—they come in many guises. Spirits by their very nature do not lend themselves easily to a factual accounting, yet in sultry Louisiana, apparitions are the norm. With a reputation for possessing more ghostly inhabitants than real ones, the Bayou State boasts ghost tales that are legendary and prolific. Ghosts here do not require any manufacturing. *They just are.* Why? *They always have been.* For most residents of Louisiana, this is about all the logical explanation necessary for validation.

The spirits who roam these pages are quirky characters, displaying amazing abilities: the apparition at Loyd Hall in Cheneyville plays the violin; Madewood's poltergeist favors feats of prestidigitation; the Capitol Ghost in Baton Rouge triggers security alarms; the ghostly decorator at the Lanaux Mansion in the French Quarter offers impeccable advice; and like Alice in Wonderland, a little girl is trapped in the mirror at Lafitte Guest House on Bourbon Street.

The television documentary *The Haunting of Louisiana* was intended as a showcase for a few of these restless souls. With layer upon layer of ghostly phenomena wandering about, some spirits did not get to prance before the camera—after all a one-hour television program has its limitations. A book format provides more spacious accommodations for these spectral creatures to strut their stuff. Once free, they populated my world. A caveat for the reader: they are poised to take over yours; a belief in the supernatural is not a prerequisite.

The stories gathered here are sprinkled with a few personal notes and observations. Enjoy.

Acknowledgments

I am thankful for all of the readers, independent bookstores, gift shops, and libraries who have been loyal fans of *The Haunting of Louisiana* over the years. I have enjoyed meeting you at author talks and book signings.

Haunted tales and ghost stories are not just for Halloween. They are part of our shared culture; they keep the past alive and remind us of who came before. So, I hope you will also enjoy *The Haunting of Mississippi* and my newest endeavor, *The Haunting of Cape Cod and the Islands*. I am excited that Pelican Publishing is now releasing companions to these titles in Arcadia and the History Press's popular *Haunted America Series*.

All creative endeavors are collaboration. I am gratefully indebted to those who shared their stories with me: Naomi Marshall and Keith Marshall, Madewood Plantation; Edith Layton, Ormond Plantation; Marion Hebert, Destrehan Manor; Louis Cornay, Chretien Point; Anne Fitzgerald and Beulah Davis, Loyd Hall; Foster Creppel, Woodland Plantation; Phillip J. Jones, Mary Louise Prudhomme, John Hoover, Wanda Lee Porter, and David Bonaventure, the Old State Capitol; Capt. Jerome Dupré, Chacahoula Tours; Tom Duran, New Orleans Ghost Tours; Ruth Bodenheimer, Lanaux Mansion; Danny O'Flaherty, O'Flaherty's Irish Channel Pub; Kevin Kelly and Jim Blanchard, Houmas House; Debra and Zeb Mayhew, Jr., Oak Alley; and Richard Naberschnig, Magnolia Lane.

Special thanks go to Nina Kooij, editor in chief at Pelican Publishing, who guided me through my first book and has been here through all that followed. A few of the lively spirits in this book first appeared in a television feature I produced for Peggy Scott Laborde's weekly show, *Steppin' Out*–many thanks, Peggy. A decade later, I expanded the idea into a full-length documentary, *The Haunting of Louisiana*, that aired on PBS stations around the country. Thanks also to Joslyn Yeager, former program director of WLAE-TV, for her wise counsel and encouragement. To Bill Yeager, I truly appreciate your thoughtful reading and comments. As always, to Glinda and Tom Schafer, I couldn't do any of it without you. And for this go-round, many thanks to Tom Chartrand of Shoreline Digital Productions.

To Danielle Genter Moore, Rebecca Genter, and Heather Genter, who always offer their unconditional support–I am indeed fortunate to have such talented and tolerant daughters. A special thanks to Danielle for your expert research and for your inspiring photographs. To Rebecca, your patience and persistence, reading and rereading every word, held me to a higher standard. I would still be wandering aimlessly among my contentious spirits without your talent and skill. I live for your checkmarks of approval!

Any liberties taken with noted figures of the past are all mine. If I have erred, I am confident their spirits will find a way to come back and haunt me. Some of the owners of these historic sites have changed, but the ghosts remain as intriguing as ever.

HAUNTED LOUISIANA

The Cajun loup garou, *in a scene from the documentary* The Haunting of Louisiana.

1

Ile Phantom

Deep inside the murky labyrinth of Louisiana's coastal wetlands, swamp creatures of mythical proportions populate both Native American and Cajun lore. *"The loup garou, the feu follet, the coquin l'eau, the will-o'-the-wisp* . . . all the monsters live on that island right there."* As he skillfully guides his flatboat through overgrown logging canals, veteran captain Jerome Dupré points to their favorite haunt.

Ile Phantom, Ghost Island, is a minuscule spit of land floating among the marsh grasses of Bayou Segnette. Curtains of dusky Spanish moss dangle from haggard branches. Overhead a great blue heron circles the island, watching for movement below. Slithering through a mangled web of knobby cypress knees, a seven-foot gator slips into the tepid water. Palmetto thickets dotting the shoreline offer impenetrable hideaways for deadly water moccasins. Owls, turtles, nutria, raccoons, snowy egrets, ibis, wood ducks—all are mindful of the dangers within, and without. The wildlife of *Ile Phantom* is on alert for the traps and nets of marauding mortals seeking tidbits for their succulent gumbos. They pay little heed, however, to the ragtag band of ghosts and monsters, who seem intent on keeping humans off their island.

Dressed in baggy denim coveralls, a battered straw hat, and white fisherman's boots, Jerome Dupré is happiest trekking through the swamps on a quest for slumbering alligators. The man with the graying ponytail traces his lineage back to the original settlers of Acadiana. *Les Acadiens* arrived in the Bayou Lafourche area in 1785; they came from France, via a little side trip to Nova Scotia in Canada. These ancestors, along with their Native American neighbors, passed on tales of the legendary creatures who live on *Ile Phantom.*

On a "scary" scale the captain rates the *loup garou,* the Cajun werewolf, as especially dangerous. Dupré's lyrical Cajun accent flows like a looping roller coaster, each word hooking a ride with one that came before. When spoken by Dupré, *loup garou* eases into the more melodious-sounding *rougarou.* He also favors tongue-in-cheek Cajun-French logic: *je pensee, les ton passé les ton passé, quoique, que'qu'chose rester les meme* (I think, the time passes even though some things stay the same).

When dealing with the devilish loup garou Dupré urges caution, for the Cajun werewolf is capable of changing himself into any form at will. As a small child, the captain remembers being warned by his parents: "If you gonna go to Grandma's house, now you stay on that path. Now don't you step off that path because if you go out there to pick yourself a pretty flower, it can be a *rougarou.* And the *rougarou* is gonna change himself. He's gonna bite you on the neck, and you're gonna spend the rest of your life dancing with the other were-wolves on Bayou Goula."

Captain Dupré tried the same warning on his own children, hoping, like his parents, to instill a little healthy fear of the real dangers inherent in the bayou. But the younger generation, says Dupré, think they are immune and far too sophisticated to believe in supernatural monsters. What they fail to understand, feels Dupré, is that stories of creatures who change forms and attack humans have been around for a long time and are shared by many cultures. The *loup garou* is a werewolf with a Cajun twist; he hangs out in the swamp, hairy arms oozing with mud. Rising on his hind legs, he bares his considerable fangs, seeking the warm blood of his next victim.

Another denizen of the brackish marsh is one Captain Dupré dubs the *coquin l'eau.* "It's a water devil. I can't recall anybody ever seeing a *coquin l'eau,* but *coquin* is like a devil—

it's a type of devil in French—and *l'eau* is the water. So he lives in that water," and, warns the captain, "he'll do sneaky things to you. You might have yourself a real good meal, a fine repast and drink a glass of wine, or two or three bottles, and if you walk outside the house, he's the thing that trips you over, pushes you off the walk, makes you fall in the bayou. That's *coquin l'eau* that do that," nods the captain. "I understand," he says with a straight face, "that they're extending their range throughout the world." Dupré allows that *coquins l'eau* can have their pluses as far as monsters go. "It's nice to have them around. One night my buddy and I, we protected our family all night long. We couldn't hit them with full beer cans, but we could hit the *coquins l'eau* with empty beer cans. So we worked on that pretty good." Dupré spins yarns at dizzying speeds, from terrifying look-over-your-shoulder tales to I'm-pulling-your-leg-see-if-you-can-keep-up whoppers. The truth darts somewhere just below the surface.

Superstition cuts hefty inroads into Cajun beliefs and practices. Parents of young children are told to be particularly wary of the *feu follet* and to keep a stash of mustard seeds on hand to hold him at bay. Sitting in a cane rocker in his cabin near the bayou, twin baby alligators tucked under each arm, Captain Dupré shares his knowledge of the terrible *feu follet*. As Dupré weaves this supernatural tale, he works his own magic on the baby alligators; short, gentle strokes under the chin induce a somnolent state in the small creatures with the large teeth, a state in which they remain until the tale is over.

"The *feu follet* is supposed to be a child's spirit, a child still suckling from its mother when it died. It's an uncomfortable spirit. The *feu follet* is restless. What happens is that the Cajuns used to think that if their children would wake up with rosy [cheeks], that the *feu follet* had gotten into the room and was suckling on the children's breath." Captain Dupré continues to rock and stroke. The alligators' eyes are at half-mast and their closed mouths form smirky grimaces, wrapping from one side of their elongated snouts to the other; the effect is chilling. The fluid voice of the captain pulls the listener into a similar trance, as he explains how Cajun parents try to protect their children from this supernatural fiend who would suck the life's breath from their babies. To foil the evil *feu follet,* a traditional method of preventive medicine was carefully laid out. "What they did was scatter mustard seeds all around and underneath the bed. Before the *feu follet* could get to the children, it had to count all the mustard seeds."

The name of the inventive parent who first struck this bargain has been lost to the annals of folklore, but according to Dupré, forcing the child-snatching *feu follet* to count the mustard seeds saved many an innocent infant. "Mustard seeds are so tiny, like a speck of black pepper. And even if the *feu follet* got close to gitting all the count, he'd lose count, and he'd have to start all over again. So he couldn't get to the children."

Dupré stops his hypnotic massage and the limp bodies of the alligators snap back to life. Leaning over, he places the twin terrors into a large wicker basket resting on the wide planks of the cabin floor. Queried as to how he knows so much about the *feu follet,* he instantly responds, "O my God, I heard it since I was old enough to know that there was a *feu follet. Feu follet* is exactly like a *will-o'-the-wisp;* it slips in and out so fast, you can hardly see it. *Feu follet,*" pronounces the captain, is "like a fire spirit moving in the sky."

This talented raconteur launches into a personal narrative about the *feu follet.* "I remember this old Black woman telling my mama . . ." The captain's story swerves now on a momentary detour. "We owned part of Delacroix Plantation down the Mississippi River. As a matter of fact, when we plowed the fields, we'd dig up spoons. They were so soft, they were made so pure of silver, you could wrap 'em up and curl 'em up like this." The captain demonstrates, taking an imaginary spoon and folding it into a ring around his finger. "Every now and then we'd dig up swords. Apparently there was some type of battle there, you know, a skirmish that took place, with all the horseshoes and the iron that we dug up. It was the original site of the antebellum plantation for the Delacroix family."

Dupré shoves a few wiry gray hairs off his face, getting back on track. "We had some enormous oak trees in the front of the house, possibly 300 years old. The old Black lady, she told my mama, she said: *'Look one night; you're gonna see a light in those oak trees. You going to see a light coming through that tree up there and it's gonna be Mr. Delacroix, and he's gonna show you where the money is buried.'*"

Captain Dupré knows how to reel in his listeners with the best of them: a ghost *and* buried treasure—a captivating combination. "So one night, my dad wasn't there and here comes, we can see a light comin' through the trees. My mama put all the lights out in the house and made the children get underneath the beds. She was afraid, you know, that a spirit was out there. My mom was from Alabama; she wasn't familiar with all this voodoo stuff," though Dupré says his father's family had indoctrinated the children well. "We loved to be scared. They didn't have television until the midfifties so we would listen to the radio at night. We'd be listening to *The Inner Sanctum*, *Sam Spade*—so family stories of the *rougarou*, the *feu follet*, the *coquin l'eau*—all of those went together."

Years later, says the captain, he asked his mother why she told the children to hide under the bed when she saw the *feu follet*. Her reply to her son was that "she was just teasing and it was the moon coming through the trees." Captain Dupré does not buy his mother's explanation. "It doesn't seem like such a tease to me, you know. She didn't get out from under the bed and turn on the light until my dad got home."

And what about those tales of buried treasure? Back aboard his boat cruising by *Ile Phantom*, the Cajun captain regales tourists on his "Chacahoula Swamp Tour" with the exploits of local hero/villain Jean Lafitte. "Ghost Island got its name because the pirate Jean Lafitte supposedly cut someone's throat and buried them on the island. Now, the legend goes that wherever Jean Lafitte buried treasure, he also buried a man with it. The thing is, it's best to stay on his good side, you know, if you wanted to live and not be buried." Dupré gives an insider's view of the nefarious pirate's double dealing.

"He [Jean Lafitte] is thinking if he killed one of his men and buried him there along with the treasure, they'd protect that treasure." Dupré pulls the throttle back to a full stop; the bow of the boat nudges the bank of *Ile Phantom*, placing the tourists dangerously close to the pirate's former lair.

The periphery of the island is marked by the stark white trunks of dying cypress trees, barren arms outstretched, beseeching the heavens for mercy. Salt-water intrusion from the Gulf, and the nutria with its voracious appetite for vegetation, have combined in a two-pronged attack on the delicate ecosystem of Louisiana's wetlands. The sudden "caw, caw, cawing" of a swooping black hawk heightens the ominous atmosphere. Dupré returns to the topic of ghosts. "You know, they'd be pretty mean 'bout having to die for that treasure. They claim people going on *Ile Phantom*, stepping on this island, looking for treasure, have been run off by ghosts, and the ghosts are dressed in pirate-type attire, turn-of-the-century clothing. The ghosts are dripping with seaweed and they run the people off. The treasure hunters would leave quickly for fear of their life."

All in all this is a plausible scenario for why treasure has never been found on *Ile Phantom*—or elsewhere in these parts. Dupré indicates a wide channel leading away from the island. "Bayou Segnette right here was the main path that Jean Lafitte came from his warehouses, hidden in the bayous, into the city of New Orleans."

Dupré paints a less-than-appealing picture of the dashing folk hero who sold smuggled goods at cut-rate prices to New Orleans' Creoles. "They loved him. He didn't pay taxes, so he gave them a great price on all his goods."

As to what happened to the legendary Jean Lafitte, the captain shrugs, lifting his shaggy eyebrows. "There are two different legends. One for sure is that when he was run out of Barataria Bay back here, he set up shop in Galveston, Texas, and there are some who claim to be his descendants still living there. Another legend has him going to Central America and that he died capturing prizes."

The least-likely version Captain Dupré repeats is that Lafitte "moved to Missouri incognito and spent the rest of his life writing his memoirs." Captain Dupré says he'd be the first person in line to read them—if they ever come on the market.

Like so many businesses, Capt. Jerome Dupré's Chacahoula Bayou Tours did not reopen after Hurricane Katrina. However, as long as there are visitors brave enough to navigate Louisiana's haunted bayous, boat tours will eagerly take you there. *Ile Phantom* (Ghost Island) will continue to harbor its spirits deep in the marsh grasses of Bayou Segnette, and the ghost of the pirate Jean Lafitte may lurk in the shadows along with the elusive *loup garou.*

Spirit bottles hanging from an oak tree in front of Magnolia Lane.

2

The Locked Room

Spirit bottles dangle from the craggy limbs of oak trees. The practice of hanging spirit bottles traces its origins to early Afro-Caribbean voodoo traditions, where the belief holds that the clanging of water-filled bottles against tree branches will ward off evil spirits. Magnolia Lane, a West Indies-style house, has been in the Naberschnig/Quinette family for over a century. Richard Naberschnig reinstated the ritual of the bottles in the 1970s when strange noises and mysterious apparitions plagued the house, particularly one bedroom in the front.

"All my life my mother kept that door, the door to that room, locked because she said that's a bad room. My mother was very superstitious. She was well educated, graduated from Newcomb College, but she was superstitious about this room because so many people died in that bed." Dressed casually in open-collared blue shirt and jeans, a white-haired Richard sits on the top step leading to the house and looks back over his shoulder. "No one ever stayed in that room in my entire life until I stayed there." He is referring to a bedroom known to Naberschnig family members as the "Dying Room." Richard's son goes through the tally. "My great-great-grandparents, my great-grandparents, and my grandparents all died in the room." Richard's mother, Grace, ordered the room to be locked and shuttered, believing it was somehow cursed.

After a twenty-year absence, Richard Naberschnig returned to his family home, hoping the curse had lifted, but not even the spirit bottles he'd strung in the trees could work their magic. "In 1976, I moved back into the house from across the river. And when I came back I unlocked the room and was sleeping in the bed. I was the first person to sleep in there in fifty years. This was the only place I could sleep 'cause my mother was across the hallway in the original bedroom. First night, at eleven o'clock, I was in this room, and I heard some loud heavy breathing in the corner like *huuhh, huuhh, huuhh*. And it scared me half to death, OK? The second night the same thing happened again. I said, 'Whoever you are I'm staying here. You can keep doing whatever you're doing.'" Squatting next to Richard, his dog, Muscles, a scruffy German Shepherd mix, moans as if to underscore the unsettling nights spent in the room. Richard ruffles the dog's fur and gives him a reassuring hug. "Yes, Muscles, that's how it goes."

Magnolia Lane, located near Westwego, is a curious amalgam of architectural styles. Built in 1784 for Edward Fortier with a hipped roof, the exterior is classic West Indian plantation style. Yet, the interior with its wide central hall has an Anglo-American floorplan. "There is a certain thing about the house. I'll walk around at night, and I'll feel as though I feel my mother. It was my mother's house. I feel that she is still here, and I will get goosebumps on my arms. And I do feel that certainly the house is occupied with people other than myself."

Richard steps into the now unlocked "Dying Room." Dominating the large space is a massive matching bedroom suite consisting of a nineteenth-century mahogany bed, armoire, and dresser. Richard's gaze rests on a cluster of framed pictures on a small oval table under the window. The window itself features just a few of the 809 glass panes original to the house. The first picture he holds is of his mother, Grace, who died in the house. He identifies the second photo of a small child: "My father, Robert Mitchell Naberschnig, with his little dog. See how a boy would dress in a dress? He was born in 1898 so this was taken in 1900, I would guess. He died in this room."

Richard picks up the final photo and strokes it. "This is my aunt Lottie, who died in the Mississippi River out front. And back then you could cross the river only by ferry, and my family operated the ferry, the Oak Street ferry. And all it was,

was a big skiff. And a ship split the boat in half. The river is very treacherous right here at Nine Mile Point because of the currents in the river, the big eddies, and the water's almost two hundred feet deep at spots. The only way you could get to New Orleans, the favorite place to go, the closest place is Oak Street and that's where she was going the night that happened." He sets the picture down gently. "So I lost my nice aunt Lottie because of that. She was just twenty-one."

It is clear from a glance around the rooms that the Naberschnig family treasures each and every object collected over the years. "This place has not changed since 1867, since we bought it. Nothing's changed. It's absolutely the same way," states Richard. "The fireplaces are for burning logs. The old loom is in here. I have a little notebook belonged to my great-grandmother; it's her grocery shopping list. Let's see what we can see: the prices on August 5, 1895. She's buying different things." He flips through the pages. "Here we go. Bread was a nickel. Eggs were thirty-five cents. Fruit was fifty-five cents, turnips were thirty cents, potatoes ten cents, beans fifteen cents, lard twenty-five cents, soap twenty cents." Richard reads another notation. "Friday December 30, steak fifteen cents, coffee sixty-five cents, tea forty-five cents." He shakes his head in amazement. "I'm always advocating, we don't get enough money for farm products, and we still don't."

Richard returns to the wide central hall and opens another door. "This is the attic staircase. It's moving up almost straight up. You have to have little narrow steps on it so it doesn't take up much room; it's a duplicate of the kind of old staircase they had in the original New Orleans French Opera house. It works very well. And when we come back down, we come backwards because we certainly don't want to fall." Richard chuckles, cocks his head upwards, and admits there's also a ghost in the attic. Although he isn't sure who the ghost is, he's seen the spectral figure up there numerous times. The sightings have convinced the owner of Magnolia Lane that "I really believe now in the spiritual world and those things."

The house and grounds of Magnolia Lane mirror the

twists and turns of the lives of the people who settled along the Great Mississippi River Road. "We had the first nursery here, maybe the oldest in this part of the country," claims a proud Richard Naberschnig. "We opened it in 1867. My family grew vegetables and sold them in the French Market in New Orleans. We grew the first orange trees in Louisiana. After that we grew oak trees here. We still do. At the end of the Civil War the trees were planted at Tulane University, City Park, Audubon Park, and along St. Charles Avenue. So all those oak trees over there in the city come from Nine Mile Point; that's where we are standing right now. Nine Mile Point is nine miles from Jackson Square; that's the seat of the government. It's a point in the river."

On what he calls his "fifty-cent tour," Richard's adult son indicates areas of peculiar occurrences on the lush grounds. "Over there is the hanging tree, and behind it is a family graveyard. They're haunted. At night things move all over the place."

Richard Naberschnig is unruffled by all things paranormal at Magnolia Lane. "I really believe in ghosts. This house is haunted, because any place that doesn't change like this hasn't for 200 years, there are likely to be some people that are still here, some spirits that are still here."

3

The Lady of Illusion

The palatial grandeur of Oak Alley Plantation reigns over the west bank of the Mississippi River in Vacherie. Lining the entrance is a commanding avenue of twenty-eight sheltering live oak trees, hailed as the most photographed avenue of trees in the world. A couple from Texas who set out to take a few souvenir photos of their own captured more than most. Their photo of the master bedroom created quite a stir.

Oak Alley's master bedroom has been restored to the period of the original owners. It was the domain of Jacques Telesphore Roman and his Creole bride, the lovely Celina. Peering over the Plexiglas barriers, tourists are able to catch a glimpse of a typical day in 1837. Sunbeams stream through the windows, showering the room with sparkling highlights. A mahogany breakfast tray rests on the carved pineapple tester bed; the lace-edged covers are turned down. The master and mistress have just finished their early-morning ritual of café au lait and sugary beignets while the newest addition to the Roman family sleeps peacefully in his elaborate rosewood cradle. In the far corner, a mannequin is draped in the mistress's latest outfit, awaiting madam's pleasure.

Mesmerized by the scene before them, Mr. and Mrs. Larry Bernard of Fort Worth, Texas quickly snap several pictures, hoping to capture the magical scene. They are wildly successful. One photo reveals the figure of a slight young woman serenely standing and staring out of the French doors to the avenue of oaks below. Masses of thick dark hair cascade down her back.

Closer examination of the snapshot does little to explain the

Oak Alley's Legendary "Lady Of Illusion"

The Bernards' photo, replicated as a postcard, with the headless mannequin reflected in the mirror instead of the figure of a woman with a head of curly dark hair.

odd presence. She is visible in the photo, but her reflection in the mirror is minus a head. The Bernards lingered at the end of the tour; they saw no one else in the master bedroom suite when they took their pictures. The couple sent the mystifying photo back to Oak Alley, hoping the staff could offer some explanation of how a nonexistent woman posed for their camera and lost her head.

The staff could only shrug and suggest perhaps "the lady" was merely a distortion of the headless dressmaker's form. If so, where did the head adorned with dark curls come from, and how did it pop up in the photo? French revolutionaries were famous for crying, "Off with her head!"—however, this was a case study in reverse dynamics. A headless mannequin was caught with her head intact.

In Louisiana, the land of dreamy dreams, this now-you-see-her, now-you-don't "Lady of Illusion" may very well be the lovely Celina Roman, slipping back into the home she fondly called *Bon Séjour*—Pleasant Sojourn. For Celina was as entranced with the "Legacy of the Avenue of Oaks" as others had been before her.

The legacy began with a mysterious French settler. In the early 1700s, lured by the promise of colonial opulence, he built a crude cabin on this site. Dreaming one day of a palatial home, he planted twenty-eight tiny oak saplings to create a magnificent entrance. The harsh economics of rural life shattered his dream; his grand palace was not to be, and the unknown visionary faded from the scene.

By the 1830s the picture changed dramatically. Sugarcane ushered in a flow of ready cash. François-Gabriel ("Valcour") Aimé, "the Sugar King of Louisiana," purchased this tract of land, which travelers and steamboat captains dubbed "Oak Alley" after the now-imposing quarter-mile avenue of towering oaks. In 1836, Valcour, brother-in-law of Celina's husband, Jacques, made the newlyweds an offer they couldn't refuse.

The enthusiastic couple purchased the coveted land and plunged into building their dream home. Only the best would do. Celina's father, the architect Gilbert Joseph Pilié, designed a home for his daughter that would mirror the grandeur of the legendary oaks. Pilié surrounded the house with twenty-eight classic Doric columns—one column for each of the twenty-eight trees—a tribute to the nameless creator of "Oak Alley." Sadly, like the unknown settler before her, Celina's stay in this place of tranquil beauty was short-lived.

Tragedy struck in 1848. Celina's beloved husband, Jacques, died, a victim of tuberculosis. The widow Celina was devastated. Unable to cope with the management of a large country estate, she was forced to sell. The plantation went on the auction block, lost forever to the Roman family.

Oak Alley's director of marketing, Debra Mayhew, is skeptical when it comes to ghosts. Her husband, executive director Zeb Mayhew, Jr., also had doubts until one fateful evening. "It was about five years ago," Debra Mayhew recalls. "The weather was really, really bad. At one o'clock in the morning the alarm went off in the mansion. Zeb went to check it out. Upstairs in the children's bedroom the door to the gallery was open. The wind blew the rain inside the room. So, he proceeded downstairs to get a mop, and when he got to the third to last step he felt somebody push him, and he fell down the last three steps onto his knees. He turned around to look back up the staircase and said, 'Don't do that to me again.' When Zeb told me about it, he said, '*Somebody* pushed me. I didn't trip.'" Debra Mayhew has an idea who the agitated spirit might be. "Mrs. Stewart, the last owner; she bought Oak Alley in 1925 and she died in the house in 1972. A lot of our guides have seen her in her bedroom sitting on the end of the bed when they bring tours in the room."

If former owner Josephine Stewart is a little put out over all the strange people in her home, it is understandable. If Celina Roman is indeed the spectral "Lady of Illusion" admiring the impressive avenue of oaks below, who can blame her? And if visitors, tour guides, and staff swear that ghosts frequently stop by, Debra Mayhew has concluded that people who are true believers in the paranormal cannot be swayed.

4

The Pesky Poltergeist

A lively spirit indulges in startling feats of prestidigitation at Madewood, a Greek Revival manor house gracing the banks of Bayou Lafourche in Napoleonville. The dining room is this spirit's favorite spot for staging his flamboyant displays.

New Orleans gallery owner and art consultant Naomi Marshall purchased Madewood in 1964 and immediately set about restoring the main house to its former glory. The original construction of the 1840s mansion spanned four years, utilizing over sixty thousand bricks. The temple-like façade features six fluted Ionic columns and diamond-shaped balusters wrapping the upper gallery.

Resplendent in a deep-purple suit, gleaming white hair precisely coifed, eighty-year-old Naomi Marshall regally held court in the parlor, recalling the monumental task of removing decades of debris from the home's interior. The pigeon droppings and accumulated mold were so encrusted on the walls and ceilings that Naomi determined the only practical method to clean house was to take a hose to it.

One day early in the cleaning process stood out from the rest. Naomi remembered wearing a bathing suit, head wrapped in a kerchief, spraying water up the carved interior stairwell, when a man drove up and said, "I'd love to see the house." Graciously, Naomi obliged. She put down her hose and invited him inside. As they stood under the peeling ceiling and crumbling walls, their conversation revealed how perilously close Madewood had come to meeting a permanent demise.

The stranger announced: "I'm sorry you got this house before I could."

The Pugh family cemetery, whose spirits do not like to be disturbed.

Curious Naomi inquired, "What would you have done with it?"

Shaking his head in profound regret over his loss, the stranger responded: "The money I could have gotten for the brick and timber."

Naomi Marshall wasted no time ushering the demolition expert to the door, informing him that his "tour was over."

To some, progress is tearing down and moving forward. To most in Louisiana, progress is ensuring that the past is alive and well and that there is always a place at the table for family—even the dearly departed.

When Naomi Marshall signed the papers for Madewood, she bought it lock, stock—and cemetery. Although she was pleased to find that it came replete with the original Pugh family tombs, she had not counted on one of the deceased joining them for dinner.

Guarded by an ancient army of stalwart oaks, the Pugh family cemetery lies tucked about three hundred yards behind the main house. Dripping from gnarled limbs, tendrils of graying Spanish moss caress the tips of the tallest tombs. A gentle breeze wafts to and fro. Defying gravity, a rust-speckled iron fence leans precariously inward, as if unseen hands are gathering it close to protect the family's last vestige of privacy. Since 1846, Col. Thomas Pugh, his wife, Elizabeth Foley, their children, and their children's children have slept here side by side, their whispered secrets caught in the languid air.

While Naomi and her family wisely left the tombs themselves untouched, they did clear away mounds of tangled weeds and rotting wood. One disgruntled soul, possibly Colonel Pugh himself, was clearly not pleased with the new unobstructed view, and the ensuing visitors. A little retaliation, it seems, was in order. To make his objections known, the ghost decided to see how the Marshalls would react to a little rearrangement at one of *their* family gatherings.

Naomi Marshall described the evening when the grumpy ghost commanded their attention with unusual table manners. "We were all sitting around talking and laughing after a big dinner. I had a magnificent cranberry epergne [glass centerpiece] on the buffet. All of a sudden the epergne just lifted up and came down on the floor." Mrs. Marshall raised her arms to demonstrate the levitation of the priceless family heirloom.

Fortunately for the Marshalls the ghost was not too vindictive, carefully avoiding any permanent damage. "It was amazing," declared Naomi. "Not a chip was broken off of it."

Despite the dramatic display of disapproval by the pesky poltergeist, the Marshalls remained convinced that their restoration efforts have ensured Madewood's very survival for future generations to enjoy. Colonel Pugh's portrait now hangs prominently in a downstairs hallway; neither the Marshalls nor their bed and breakfast guests have reported any recent signs of furrowed brows, frowns, disapproving signs, or, alas— to the disappointment of avid ghost lovers—any further feats of prestidigitation.

Arts patron Naomi Damonte Marshall died at the age of ninety-two. Her legacy lives on through Madewood Plantation, her children, and the careers of the many noted Louisiana artists she nurtured. Her son, Keith Marshall, and her daughter-in-law, Millie Ball, former travel editor for the *New Orleans Times-Picayune*, sold the National Historic Landmark in 2018. In an interview at the time, Keith Marshall said the sale was "bittersweet." "Millie and I have physically left Madewood, but what we achieved will remain with us forever." Fortunately, Madewood remains open to visitors. But for the sake of any remaining ghostly presence, please tread lightly, especially when wandering near the Pugh family cemetery. The Pughs are quite particular about their privacy.

5

What Else Do They Leave Behind?

By their very nature, antebellum homes are repositories of the past. Many a soul has passed through the portals of a 200-year-old plantation. The late Edith Layton, a former docent at Ormond Plantation, poses a provocative question: "With so many occupants stamping a variety of emotions upon this particular environment, if it's possible to leave fingerprints, what else is left behind?"

What else indeed? Ormond Plantation, in St. Charles Parish on the east bank of the mighty Mississippi near Destrehan, is full of dark secrets. Completed in 1790, the Louisiana colonial-style home was part of a land grant awarded to Pierre Trepagnier by the Spanish governor of the Louisiana territories, Don Bernardo de Galvez. The lavish home was often the setting for elaborate parties in honor of visiting dignitaries. In 1798 sugar baron Pierre Trepagnier vanished without a trace, leaving his children haunted by a father they would never know.

One evening while the Trepagniers were at dinner, a servant entered the room to inform the master that a coach with a Spanish insignia on the door had driven up to the property. Pierre got up to see. When the servant checked, his master and the phantom coach had mysteriously disappeared. No trace of Pierre Trepagnier was ever found, although one medium feels she may have been in contact.

In the 1990s, the restored Ormond Plantation once again played gracious host and was the scene for a special function for visiting hospitality-industry executives. As part of the evening's

A mysterious carriage appeared at Ormond Plantation and drove off with owner Pierre Trepagnier, never to be seen again.

entertainment, a voodoo demonstration and seance were in progress. The china and silverware on the dining-room table were removed, and the medium spread her accoutrements across the polished mahogany surface. In the center of the table, she placed a small incense dish to ward off evil spirits. To set the proper period mood for the guests, Edith Layton, Ormond's business manager, donned full antebellum finery—blue taffeta bouffant gown, red hair piled high, cameo necklace on black-velvet ribbon—the quintessential Southern dame. Lighting the candles, Edith began with the tale of Pierre Trepagnier's untimely disappearance. "When I got to the part about Pierre walking out the door and his family never seeing him again, the little incense dish cracked with a loud pop, right on cue." Smiling Edith Layton adds, "I thought it was effective."

Other masters of Ormond Plantation seemed doomed to follow the tragic fate of Pierre. On June 25, 1805, Col. Richard Butler bought the house and land from the widow Trepagnier. He rechristened the home Ormond, taking the name from his ancestral property, the Castle Ormonde in Ireland. Colonel Butler did not have long to savor his latest acquisition. Terrified by the dreaded yellow fever that was ravaging the local populace, he sold Ormond in 1819, fleeing with his wife to what he believed was the healthier climate of Bay St. Louis, Mississippi—but escape was futile. The fever followed and took Richard Butler in his prime, at forty-three.

Ormond drifted through a series of owners after the War Between the States. In 1898, Louisiana state senator Basile LaPlace, Jr., hoped to transform Ormond into a profitable rice-producing operation. Less than a year later, he made an untimely and gruesome exit. On October 11, 1899, the senator's body, hit by a barrage of bullets, was found hanging from a massive oak tree hugging a curve on the Great Mississippi River Road.

Edith Layton says local legends differ regarding the perpetrators of the crime. "Some feel because of his political position, the senator made an enemy in the Ku Klux Klan, and the Klan killed him. Others think he was philandering with the caretaker's daughter, and it was the caretaker and his son that sought revenge." Ms. Layton states that these theories have never been proven. The only facts not in dispute are the unfortunate deaths of three men, their harrowing exits all preceded by their entrance into Ormond's hallowed halls. Ormond's ominous history is layered with tragic tales of hauntings by hapless victims and with baffling paranormal phenomena.

One of Edith Layton's personal favorites has an ironic twist. "I was leading a group of ladies on tour, and one lady in particular kept asking me about ghosts. I decided to humor her and tell her some of things that I had heard. Every time I would pause, she would punctuate the sentence by declaring, 'That's a ghost for you!' as if she was on familiar terms with every ghost who ever wandered by."

Edith's husky voice drops to a conspiratorial tone as she divulges what happened next. "At this point we're standing on the verandah and to my right I hear this deafening noise. I turned my head away while the lady is still talking, which is extremely rude, and look down the porch to see what's making the racket. Pretty soon the noise roars towards us. Something goes *through* me. My knees buckle. My mind is going, *What's that? What's that?*"

Edith says on recovering, she spun back around to check on the ladies. They appeared unscathed by the strange phenomenon. "Here this lady is still blithering on about her knowledge of the spirit world, and she hasn't heard or felt a thing." Edith's booming laugh highlights the absurdity of her predicament.

Edith Layton no longer works as a full-time tour guide; she leaves the ghost hunting to others. "People would ask me, 'Is this house haunted?' and I would normally reply, 'They work a different shift!'" Or so Ms. Layton fervently hopes, for the ghosts at Ormond, as elsewhere in Louisiana, have their own agenda, unencumbered by time and space.

6

A Finger-Pointing Ghost
and Buried Treasure

Shimmering slivers of moonbeams pierce the canopy of oaks circling the old manor house. A burst of chill air blows in from the river, lifting the craggy branches and shaking the leaves in an eerie ballet. Two deckhands clamber up the levee, returning to a tug moored on the river embankment. Glancing over his shoulder, the younger of the two speculates on what he'd do if he owned a plantation like the one behind them. "I'd sit out there on that porch, put my feet up, snap my fingers for somebody to fetch me a drink, and count my money!"

"And you'd need a lot of it if you lived there," *counters his companion, clutching his windbreaker tighter around his ample chest.*

"What is your problem, Joe? Wouldn't you like to be rich for once in your life?"

"Yeah, but I wouldn't want me a big monster house like that one. There wouldn't be enough money in the world to keep fixing the leaks in the roof and replacing the bricks on all those damn chimneys every time a hurricane roared by."

"You know what, Joe? I bet if someone handed you a treasure map right now, you'd complain about how you'd have to go get a shovel, dig a lot of holes, move a bunch of dirt, and when you finally found the treasure, then you'd complain some more, because you'd have to hire somebody to guard it 'cause people would want to steal it." *The young deckhand is feeling pretty cocky after a night on the town and enjoys ribbing his pessimistic friend.*

The two drinking buddies have taken a zigzag route to the top of the levee. The lights from the wheelhouse of the tugboat Cruisin' Cajun *illuminate the stretch of riverbank in front of the old plantation. Looking out at the muddy waters as they rest at the top of the levee, Joe nudges Rene.* "Hey, dreamer, next you're gonna tell me that patch of fog on the river is some kind of spook or ghost."

41

The ghost of the pirate Jean Lafitte pointing to buried treasure.

Rene squints in the direction Joe is looking, about fifty yards out.
"Well, it does have kind of a weird shape to it."

"Man, you're nuts." Joe plods downhill towards the string of barges
guarded by the tug.

"Joe, wait. Wait! The fog thing, one part of it is sticking out . . . like
. . . a hand. . . . I'm serious . . . it's like it's pointing to the big house . . .
maybe there's some buried treasure there!"

An impatient captain steps out of the wheelhouse, watching his
overdue deckhands stagger back. "What are you two yammering
about? The wind is picking up and I need you to check the lines."

Hustling on board, Joe nods his head back to Rene. "Oh, Boy
Wonder there is seein' things. Ghosts walking on water."

The captain fixes a hard stare at the river, then as if his head is
stuck on a rusty turret, he cranks it starboard in jerky increments
till his eyes zero in on the old plantation house. "I've had my fill of
ghosts and buried treasure," grumbles the captain. Wheeling his
considerable frame back to port, he announces, "Nobody ever found
anything." Abruptly slamming the door of the wheelhouse behind him,
the captain leaves his deckhands puzzled over his curious remarks.

Destrehan Manor, on the east bank of the river above New
Orleans, is the oldest documented plantation house in the
lower Mississippi Valley. Under the guardianship of the River
Road Historical Society, the former private home is open to
the public. Costumed docents warmly welcome most visitors,
but a ban on ghosts is strictly enforced.

The prohibition on apparitions is purely a practical one.
While other historic sites capitalized on the marketing appeal
of their alleged haunted status, rumors of a finger-pointing
ghost nearly destroyed Destrehan Manor.

Peering from behind a black veil and bonnet, *de rigueur*
accessories for her eighteenth-century mourning costume,
former museum docent Marion Hebert is visibly upset.
"Destrehan is the only plantation I know of that has suffered
damage, physical damage, from a ghost."

Fueled by a local legend of the phantom pirate Jean Lafitte
purportedly pointing to a secret cache of buried treasure,
looters went on a rampage, nearly annihilating the historic

structure in their quest for gold. Ascending the staircase, the fiercely protective docent denounces the grave impact on Destrehan as "rape." Leading the way to an unrestored second-floor bedroom, Marion demonstrates what the house looked like when the vandals were done. The *bousillage* (mud and moss insulation) was left exposed; holes were dug in the floors and ceilings; marble mantels were ripped out. The entire home was in danger of collapse, all because of an oft-repeated tale of a finger-pointing ghost.

"The story I heard," says Ms. Hebert, her black gown sweeping behind, "is the ghost of the pirate Jean Lafitte is in the house pointing to the fireplace, showing where he buried his treasure." Adjusting the lace-edged veil in front of her face, Marion laughs. "To me that story is absolutely silly. I mean, if you had money, you wouldn't hide it inside a plantation, go off, and then come back later expecting it would still be there. Surely somebody's going to find that. We all remember when the Yankees were coming. People back then ran out and buried their silver, jewels, and money in the yard thinking they [the Yankees] were too stupid to find it. We all know better than that!"

Marion Hebert is clearly not impressed with the flawed tactics of her Southern ancestors. Nor does Marion think it logical that any self-respecting ghost, especially the one of the crafty pirate Jean Lafitte, would randomly appear in front of strangers and let them know today was their lucky day. Gathering her skirts to begin the descent back to the first floor, Ms. Herbert underscores the futility of the vandals' efforts. "They found no treasure because it was never here." Supported by the stalwart eyes of the Destrehan family patriarch glowering down from his portrait, Marion Hebert is unwavering in her stance. "A man like Jean Noel Destrehan would never have welcomed a man of Jean Lafitte's character into his home."

In 1971 the River Road Historical Society came to the rescue of the abandoned plantation, promptly declaring it a "Ghost-Free Zone." Intent on preserving her historic integrity, society members swore misguided treasure hunters would never again tear her apart.

That's it then, end of story? No pirate (dead or alive) on the premises? No buried treasure?

Unfortunately for the preservationists, vehement denials did little to alleviate the rumors. The specter of the pirate Jean Lafitte hovering over Destrehan led many in the community, like the tugboat captain and his deckhand, to believe that a chest filled with sparkling gems and gold doubloons was within their grasp, if only they were the first to find it.

Jean Lafitte biographer Lyle Saxon cautions that the centuries-old quest for Lafitte's lost treasure encompasses the entire thousand-mile stretch of the Gulf of Mexico, covering "every bay, inlet and bayou from Key West to the mouth of the Rio Grande." Chances of pinpointing the exact location are slim, but for diehards, as long as there is ghost lore to follow, there is hope.

Unquestionably, having endured a series of dramatic reincarnations, Destrehan Manor, the Grand Dame of the Great Mississippi River Road in St. Charles Parish, possesses a certain mystique. From 1802 to 1910, she was home to generations of the wealthy Destrehan family. Like other Southern plantations during the Civil War, she was seized and occupied by Union forces. In 1866, the house and grounds reverted back to the Destrehans. One of Jean Noel Destrehan's daughters, Louise, and her second husband, Judge Pierre Rost, managed to revive the sugarcane operation. Yet, the end of an era was near. On Louise's death in 1877, her son Emile tried his hand at managing the complex, but poor health hampered his good intentions. Emile sold Destrehan Plantation in 1910, marking the end of the family's ownership of Destrehan Manor, and its status as a leading producer of sugarcane.

All, however, was not lost. Destrehan's enormous size and prime location facing the river appealed to a new industry. An oil refinery sprouted up over the indigo and sugarcane fields; the manor house itself functioned as an office complex and company headquarters. Destrehan Plantation adapted to the changing times. But in 1958, after 168 years of use, the aging home was deemed obsolete. Hope faded.

For the next thirteen years, she lay vacant. Her derelict condition—boarded windows, broken railings, peeling plaster, exposed bricks—cast a depressing pall over the area.

In *Gumbo Ya-Ya: Folk Tales of Louisiana*, Lyle Saxon insists that such a brooding environment is the perfect breeding ground for haunted tales: "Of course every old plantation home in Louisiana has at least one ghost."

The River Road Historical Society disputes Saxon's theory; they believe that the plantation's honored legacy is sufficiently appealing without a pirate ghost on board. Behind Destrehan's restored 1839 Greek Revival facade lies a wealth of drama.

Beginning in 1787 Frenchman Robert Antoine Robin de Logny hired a free mulatto named Charles to build a raised house "sixty feet in length by thirty-five feet," with a surrounding gallery, five chimneys, and a hipped roof. Charles labored by hand for three years to complete the project. For his efforts, Robin de Logny paid him "one hundred piastres, fifty quarts of rice and corn, a cow, and her calf." After the payment is recorded, there is no further mention of homebuilder Charles; he must have packed up his earnings and looked for a more lucrative line of work elsewhere.

Owner and planter Robin de Logny didn't last long either. He died in 1792, scarcely having time to enjoy his new home. Robin's son Pierre tried his hand at management, but thought better of it. In 1802, Pierre de Logny turned over the plantation to his new brother-in-law, Jean Noel Destrehan. The marriage of Jean Noel Destrehan to Pierre's sister, Celeste de Logny, joined two of the wealthiest families in the Louisiana colony.

The newlyweds' roles were preordained. Jean Noel would convert the indigo plantation into one of the most profitable sugarcane operations in the South; Celeste would raise the children. Large families were the norm in French Catholic Louisiana. Celeste complied, giving birth to fourteen babies. To make room for the growing family, two matching wings were added to the manor house in 1810.

Evidence of the aristocratic Destrehans' allegiance to their native France remains on display throughout the home. A portrait of Emperor Napoleon Bonaparte hangs in the front parlor, but another less-traditional family memento is the star attraction at this plantation-turned-museum. For favors rendered, the French emperor presented Jean Noel Destrehan with a solid white marble bathtub! The deed that prompted the strange thank-you gift remains a mystery.

As the owner of a prosperous plantation, Jean Noel Destrehan entertained lavishly and furnished his home with the latest fashions from Europe. When the French tricolor was lowered and the American stars and stripes raised, Jean Noel quickly switched gears; well versed in politics, he helped shape Louisiana's new state constitution in 1812.

Downriver in New Orleans things were also looking up for French expatriates Jean Lafitte and his older brother Pierre. From the back of a blacksmith shop on Bourbon Street, they conducted a thriving business selling stolen wares to a wealthy clientele, a clientele who happily circumvented payment of the hefty United States custom tax on imported goods.

By 1813 pirate Jean Lafitte was at the height of his success, operating in open defiance of the United States government. Biographer Saxon writes, "Weekly deliveries of contraband goods still came to New Orleans and convoys of sailing boats and swift pirogues went each week through Bayou Lafourche to the rich plantations along its banks." Door-to-door, or at least dock-to-dock, deliveries from the bayous to the river were readily available.

Former Destrehan docent Marion Hebert is positive the honorable patriarch, Jean Noel Destrehan, would never have stooped to dealing in such illicit trade. "Here's a man who's putting together the state constitution and believes in the laws that he's writing." If paragon of virtue Jean Noel was not in on any pirate scheme, then, reasoned the treasure hunters, some other family member, unencumbered by legal or ethical technicalities, must have been in contact with the pirate; why else would Jean Lafitte's ghost haunt this plantation?

Destrehan family papers hint at several candidates. In his final will, written in New Orleans on April 22, 1818, Jean Noel

Destrehan beseeches his wife, Celeste de Logny, to exert the utmost caution in supervising their nine surviving children. "If my son, Jean Etienne, continues to give himself to drink and to conduct himself badly, I implore my wife and the trustee of my younger children to instigate an interdiction against him."

It appeared that Jean Etienne was traveling in questionable circles and was in danger of losing his inheritance. Writing in *Le Communiqué,* the newsletter of the River Road Historical Society, editor Irene Tastet is hopeful that future research will provide answers on whether or not Jean Etienne Destrehan mended his ways. Bad boy or not, there is no substantial proof that Jean Etienne hooked up with any pirate—or provided a safe haven for Jean Lafitte to stash his loot.

Marion Hebert believes that the entire story of a finger-pointing ghost is a case of mistaken identity. For her, the missing link between the perfidious pirate and the plantation was neither patriarch Jean Noel nor his excommunicated son Jean Etienne, but rather Jean Etienne's brother, Nicholas Noel Destrehan. Gazing fondly at an oval portrait of the handsome Nicholas on display in the bedroom, Marion explains that in the early 1800s boys were considered men at fourteen. No longer allowed to live in the main house, they either moved into separate quarters known as *garçonnières* or were given a plantation of their own to manage. Young Nicholas chose to set up housekeeping on family lands on the west bank of the river below Destrehan, placing him in proximity to a well-traveled route of Lafitte's band of pirates, the Baratarians.

Like a mother with a wayward child, Marion is indulgent when it comes to Nicholas. She believes that the exciting exploits of the pirate were irresistible to a young boy. "Jean Lafitte would come up Barataria [Bay] and Nicholas' plantation was right there. . . . Nicholas probably admired him, you know, a dashing man. They became friends and Jean Lafitte would stop at Nicholas' plantation and visit with him."

Compounding the confusion over names, Nicholas's father's plantation on the east bank of the river and Nicholas's own on the west bank were both called Destrehan. Jean Lafitte, Jean

Noel, Jean Etienne, Nicholas Noel; Destrehan on the east bank, Destrehan on the west bank; stormy night, winding river—any ghost might get a bit confused after being on the prowl for nearly two centuries.

Acquiescing momentarily to the popular notion of a phantom pirate on the grounds, docent Hebert allows that *if* Jean Lafitte's ghost popped up at Destrehan Plantation (on the east bank; son Nicholas Noel's plantation on the west bank no longer exists), he probably just lost his bearings and wound up pointing to the wrong house, on the wrong side of the river(navigation on foggy nights can be tricky and spirits occasionally are blown off course). Under such trying circumstances, the ghost of Jean Lafitte can't possibly be held accountable if foolish mortals choose to follow him.

Contrary to the official policy of the River Road Historical Society, stories of the pirate and his treasure flourish. Adjusting the silk ribbons on her bonnet, docent Hebert admits it's difficult; visitors hear the rumors. "They're interested. Ghosts hold a fascination for most people. They ask about hauntings, and they'll say, 'I really want to see something.'" Unwittingly, Marion Hebert's solid-black Creole mourning outfit—hat, veil, gloves, dress—lends itself all too well to tales of the supernatural. Marion is dressed in character as one of the Destrehan wives who lost her husband at a young age. Marion's personal position on ghosts does veer a bit from the party line. "For a house to survive as long as this one, or any old buildings, they're going to have an essence, you know. We carry something with us, whether it's good or whether it's sad. It stays behind for a little time. I think that's what this house is filled with, the essence of many, many people." When pressed to identify a few of these entities, Marion confesses, "I am drawn to Nicholas. That's the simplest way I can put it. There's something about him that touches my heart and saddens me. I read a lot about Nicholas. He married at the age of twenty-one to a girl named Victoire Fortier. He loved her dearly. They were married for eleven years when she died. Nicholas mourned her for the rest of his life. He married again and had a family with his second wife, but he requested to be buried with Victoire in the cemetery of the Red Church up the road. On the tomb he says how much he loved her and that he would meet her again in the afterlife."

A deep sigh escapes from Marion. "Sometimes it's almost like I can feel Nicholas, his presence, his sadness." As for the ghost of the finger-pointing pirate Jean Lafitte and his treasure, Ms. Hebert shakes her head, smiles, and lowers her veil.

7

La Petite Fille and Friends

Kevin Kelly, the affable owner of Houmas House Plantation in Darrow, is perplexed over his unusual predicament. Visitors and staff describe the ghosts of his antebellum home on a daily basis, but, laughs Kelly, "I can't understand why they see them and I don't." He's prepared to be the genial host—if the two male phantoms will just show up. "I tell everybody that I go to bed at night with my favorite drink, Wild Turkey and 7UP. I have three drinks ready—one for me and two for the ghosts in the house—and I always have to drink all three."

Witnesses who have seen the male spirits declare that one is exceedingly tall, and the other appears to be dressed in uniform. "The one in uniform, he's probably a riverboat captain . . . he walks around on the rooftop, the widow's walk," says Kelly. The magnificent belvedere at Houmas House offers sweeping views of the Mississippi River, a perfect vantage point for any river pilot, real or phantom, to spend his leisure hours.

The second male figure strolls the grounds. "There is a tall, tall Black man. Very gentle and slow moving," states Houmas House historian Jim Blanchard. "When I first saw him, he went behind me, and I went, 'Who's that?' And then he walked through the wall!" Later, Blanchard understood that this ghost knew exactly where he was going. "I was redoing the cottage in the back, opening up the paneled walls that had been added on, and discovered a doorway that had been covered up. He was walking through a doorway that was original to the back cottage."

Kelly agrees that this particular ghost sticks to familiar

One ghost here has the disconcerting habit of walking through walls and fountains without getting wet. (Courtesy of Houmas House)

paths, ignoring any contemporary obstacles. "When I bought the property, I put a big circular fountain right behind the house. People tell me he walks right through the fountain but doesn't get wet."

This restless spirit is also spotted near the front portico. Blanchard adds, "There is an old Fonville Winans photograph . . . and in it is a seven-foot-tall Black man stepping off the front porch. It's an incredible spooky photograph when you think about it."

In addition to the adult spirits, a tiny specter causes considerable consternation. "Everyone describes her in the same way: she has on a blue dress with a pink ribbon in her brown hair," says a baffled Kelly. He purchased Houmas House in the spring of 2003 and immediately began a massive restoration. Along with regular updates on their progress, the workmen began reporting the sight of a little girl wandering about. She appeared so real to one electrician that he was concerned for her safety in what was then a construction zone. Often seen descending the freestanding spiral staircase inside the house and playing in the gardens, she has earned the nickname *La Petite Fille* (The Little Girl). In the early stages of his occupancy, Kelly allowed a séance to be held. "The séance people talked to her when I'm in the room," but Kelly emphasizes, "I didn't see her. I didn't hear her." The exchange between medium and spirit produced a few interesting moments. "The séance person said the ghost would like to be friendly with me, but she is afraid of me because I am so big. So I said, 'Well, how am I supposed to be friendly?'" Kelly was informed that the ghost child would like to play hide-and-seek with him. "Evidently, this is her favorite game in the yard because most people that talk about her say that's what she does."

Early owners, the Hampton, Preston, Beirne, and Miles families, all raised children at Houmas House. An antique doll's dress may hold a clue to the identity of the diminutive spirit. Blanchard relates the history of the delicate garment. "I acquired it from the Preston family through an auction.

There was a little handkerchief attached to the dress with May Preston's date of birth appliquéd on it."

May was the daughter of John Smith Preston and Caroline Hampton Preston. According to Kelly, when May became ill with yellow fever, her parents made plans to return to their family home in South Carolina. May died on the way. "Her body is in Columbia, South Carolina, but her soul," says Kelly, "is here. I am quite certain it is May Preston. She was born May 20, 1840, and died in 1848 of yellow fever. Let's put it this way. If the séance lady was right, it was May Preston, because the doll's dress belonged to May, and when the lady held up the doll's dress, the ghost supposedly asked, 'Where is my doll? I've been looking for it for a long time.'" Kelly quickly reiterates, "Of course, I've had no personal experience with her or our other ghosts."

Near the carriage archway that connects Alexandre Latil's original 1775 French provincial dwelling with the main 1840s Greek Revival mansion is a marble statue of a young girl. Barefoot with one leg crossed over the other, she sits on a child-size, ladder-back chair. Her eyes are downcast, her face pensive. Intrigued, visitors ask if she represents one of the children who lived or died in the house. Blanchard shakes his head. "It is odd that we have her here. People comment, 'How sweet.'" The statue adds a layer of mystery to the idyllic gardens. The girl appears to be merely catching her breath before popping up to join another game of hide-and-seek.

In 1858, sugar baron John Burnside acquired Houmas House from the Prestons. Fellow Irishman Kelly's lavish restoration pays homage to the Burnside era with its grand "Sugar Palace." During efforts to reacquire the original furnishings, a few items arrived with phantoms intact. Blanchard attests to an incident with an antique French clock. "The clock was reputed to be from Napoleon's collection, part of the collection that John Burnside bought. He adored this clock so much that he gave it as a wedding present to a good friend. We tracked it down and I went to Baton Rouge to pick it up." To avoid damage to the mechanism, the pendulum was removed for the return trip. "I pull up to Houmas House, turn the alarms off, and bring the clock in. The minute I set it on the dining-room mantel, it starts, *'Dong, dong, dong.'*" Blanchard is incredulous. "It shouldn't have been able to make a sound because the pendulum was not on. And then I hear voices of men all around the room as if the room is full of people. I just left the clock there, turned the alarm on, locked the doors, and said, 'I am not sleeping here tonight. I am going to New Orleans.'" Blanchard's only explanation for the phantom sounds? "The clock came home. After a hundred and something years of being gone, it let us know it's back. I get goose bumps right now just talking about it."

A haunted clock, a playful spirit, a tall specter, a ghost in the belvedere, and disembodied voices should be enough for any plantation, but Kelly wishes there was just one more. In 1964, Hollywood legend Bette Davis arrived at Houmas House to film scenes for *Hush . . . Hush, Sweet Charlotte*. "I would say that is our number-one draw; so many people come here just to see where Bette Davis stayed. They would love to see a ghost of Bette Davis. If I could get the world to believe her ghost was on this property, I'd get millions of people here a day."

Felicité Chretien shot a pirate invading her home, and his ghost may still be around.

8

The Ghost and
the Real Scarlett O'Hara

With her etch-a-sketch coastline battered by pugnacious storms from the Gulf, "trembling prairies" of vast watery-marshlands, and a café-au-lait river looping back on itself, time and place in the lands of Louisiana are freeform, an abstract painting in progress. Leaving their imprints on this flowing canvas were a lively young couple—and another conniving pirate.

They were Felicité and Hypolite Chretien. The pirate was a cohort of Jean Lafitte. He wanted her gold and jewels. She whipped out a pistol and shot him dead. Their encounter was recreated in the epic movie *Gone with the Wind*. The stairwell of Chretien Point Plantation served as the model for the Hollywood movie set where Scarlett O'Hara shot the "damyankee" as he tried to grab her mama's sewing basket.

In the real-life version at Chretien Point Plantation, after the outmaneuvered pirate collapsed in a pool of blood, his body was stashed in a secret compartment under the stairs. Former owner Louis Cornay believes that the pirate—his spirit, not his crumbling bones—may be with them still. Juggling past and present, the Cornays adapted to the occasional tinkering of their ghostly housemate, although sharing living quarters with the ghost they call "Robert" required a few adjustments.

When Louis Cornay, an interior designer, and his wife, Jeanne, a professor of English, first saw the antebellum marvel known as Chretien Point Plantation near Opelousas, they were enthralled. With its fan-shaped lunettes over the windows reminiscent of the Palace of Versailles, and Tuscan columns soaring to meet a gray slate roof, the magnificence of the home was evident, even when cloaked in cobwebs. Digging into the plantation's long history, Louis and Jeanne were soon convinced that, scene for scene, the saga of Chretien Point was surely deserving of an Oscar for "Best Screenplay Based on Original Material."

The first owners, Hypolite and Felicité Chretien, were a passionate and peculiar couple. Their antics rivaled those of the fictional characters in Margaret Mitchell's sweeping *Gone with the Wind* drama. Certainly the feisty Felicité Neda Chretien would have had little trouble upstaging the indomitable Scarlett O'Hara. Dispensing with the myth of the swooning Southern belle, Louis Cornay holds out his right hand and, with thumb tapping each finger in turn, methodically ticks off the extraordinary habits of Felicité: "She rode her horse astride like a man instead of sidesaddle like a lady was supposed to; she wore trousers instead of a skirt; she went tearing through the countryside; she smoked cigars; and she gambled." Glancing at Felicité's gilt-framed portrait adorning the mantel in the dining hall, the charming Mr. Cornay is clearly infatuated with the former lady of the manor. "Scarlett O'Hara actually had the same personality as our wonderful Felicité, *except* Felicité was a real person. She was absolutely the first liberated woman in Louisiana!"

Continuing the comparison between the two ravishing beauties, Louis Cornay comments on their effect on the opposite sex. "All the young men wanted to marry Felicité, and they courted her, just like in the movie everybody was courting Scarlett, but only one guy was smart enough to make the right offer." The impeccably groomed Mr. Cornay nods in obvious pleasure at the cunning of the "one guy" who won the hand of the untamed Felicité.

With an enticing game-show-host flourish, Louis Cornay reveals Felicité's unorthodox marriage proposal. "He was Hypolite Chretien II. He offers Felicité Neda, daughter of a Spanish nobleman, a *reverse* dowry to marry him." The usual custom, explains Cornay, called for the expectant bride's father to negotiate with various suitors until an acceptable dowry was proffered to the prospective groom. The smitten Hypolite bypassed tradition, *and* the other suitors in line, striking a bargain directly with Felicité. His inducement, according to Cornay, was "a bribe . . . the equivalent of over fifty thousand dollars in today's money!" Like the resourceful Scarlett, Felicité eyed the cash and hooked up with Hypolite. And like that of their fictional counterparts, Scarlett and Rhett, the colorful marriage of Felicité and Hypolite skirted the norm of the day. The Chretiens, husband and wife, were also daring entrepreneurs, filling the family coffers with profits from cotton and *contraband.*

Louis Cornay continues his tale of the Chretiens' foray into the black market, jumpstarting it with a fanciful encounter at the Battle of New Orleans. On January 8, 1815, Gen. Andrew Jackson assembled a mixed bag of fighting men to defend the city and defeat the British. Hypolite, still just an adventurous teenager, traveled south with a few fellow planters and signed up with Jackson's troops near Chalmette.

Waving his arms to represent the colliding American and British forces, Louis Cornay whips up a scene in the gory battle: "Hypolite is crouched in a ditch with his uncle. A guy on the American side runs in front of them. The guy takes a hit in his leg and falls. The young Hypolite crawls from the safety of the ditch—everybody's brave when they're eighteen. Hypolite drags the guy to safety, tends his wound, and gets him ready to go again. The fellow says, 'Thank you very much.' They introduce themselves and the young fellow says he's Hypolite Chretien, and the other guy says, 'My name is Jean Lafitte.'" Of course, says an excited Cornay, it's the pirate!

Biographer Lyle Saxon writes that Jean Lafitte and his gang, the Baratarians, had an ulterior motive siding with the Americans in the battle for control of New Orleans. They hoped to ease the mounting opposition to their illegal activities and gain favor as loyal patriots to the American cause.

After the American victory, the young Hypolite returned to Opelousas to oversee his cotton crops, and the pirates enjoyed their fifteen minutes of fame. With the stroke of a feathered pen, the "hellish banditti" were reborn in Gen. Andrew Jackson's reports to Pres. James Madison as "privateers" (authorized bounty hunters), and their sins were forgiven. But the honeymoon was short. The dual mantle of model citizen/ loyal patriot was an uncomfortable fit for Jean Lafitte and his merry men. The genteel citizenry of La Nouvelle-Orléans still refused to invite the pirates to dine with their wives and daughters. Incensed, Lafitte pulled up stakes and moved his band of Baratarians beyond the reach of the United States territorial authorities. He used Galveston Island, then part of the Republic of Texas, as his new base of operations.

Lafitte realized he still needed a place to sell his stolen wares to the prosperous Creole planters back in Louisiana. A solution, says Louis Cornay, was within reach. "The best thing Lafitte can figure out is to come and see his friend [Hypolite Chretien] in Opelousas, west of New Orleans. Hypolite would bring his friends here to the land he owns at Chretien Point and the pirates would bring their goods inland across the prairies of southwest Louisiana in wagons. They'd buy and sell right here."

Hypolite and Felicité's "garden parties" must have been a strange sight indeed: giant open-air garage sales held under swaying oak, cherry, pecan, and tallow trees. Proper Creole gentlemen in top hats, canes, and polished boots mingled with scruffy seamen clutching in callused hands a dowager's emerald brooch, a filigreed Celtic cross, or a diamond-encrusted tiara. The net result, according to Louis Cornay, was a mutually beneficial association. "Of course, the pirates would take their share and put it in their pockets and go away, and Hypolite would take his share, put it in his pockets, and get richer and richer and richer."

With their share of the profits, Hypolite and Felicité built a grand home in 1831 on the Coteau Ridge, overlooking Bayou Bourbeau. Besides hosting regular sales of contraband on the grounds, Chretien Point Plantation served as the center of a thriving 10,000-acre cotton operation. The fairytale life was in full bloom when Hypolite was bitten by a mosquito carrying the insidious yellow fever, and he died. Bravely Felicité stepped right in, keeping the pirate trade rolling. The astute

Felicité dug up Hypolite's stash of gold buried on the grounds (Hypolite did not believe in banks) and doubled her husband's fortune (some say via many a winning poker hand).

There are numerous theories about what happened to the Baratarians, but by the late 1830s only a small disorganized band of pirates was left operating out of Galveston Island. Cornay says the gang realized it was time to move on. "The last ones needed money, as all good pirates are always broke, and they decided to make one last run into Louisiana."

The pirates' scheme called for plunder and—murder. Their target was the wealthy widow, Felicité Chretien. Cornay wipes his glasses with a crisp, white-linen handkerchief and lowers his voice in the best storytelling tradition. "The pirates came here one night. There were seven left of Lafitte's gang, darting in and out of the trees." Cornay pauses for effect, turning his head towards the French doors. "Felicité is putting the children to bed and happens to hear a horse neigh in the front yard. She looks out and sees dark figures approaching. She goes to her dresser, opens the drawer, and grabs a handful of jewels and a pistol."

Pointing to the upper landing of the stairwell, Cornay draws a frightening picture. "Felicité is standing at the head of the stairs waiting . . . for sure, one of the pirates comes in the door and starts inching up the steps. With a single candle flickering like a spotlight behind her, Felicité rattles her jewelry, gasps, and orders the pirate not to come any further." Cornay smugly emphasizes that "Felicité was very smart—what she was really saying was 'Come a little closer; I can't see you well enough yet.'" Lured by the glittering jewels, the greedy pirate placed a muddy boot on the second ramp of steps. Felicité pulled the pistol out from behind her back and shot him dead. The unlucky pirate fell on the eleventh step.

In Louis Cornay's rendition of the events, Felicité jumped over the dead Baratarian, called for her servants, gave them rifles, and chased the rest of the gang away. The house servants took the body and hid it in the cabinet under the stairs. They scrubbed the blood from the carpet, but neglected to wash the wood underneath. This stain provided the Cornays with their first clue to the identity of the ghost haunting Chretien Point Plantation.

Over the years, Chretien Point, like so many other plantations, fell into disrepair. The vacant mansion was used by local farmers. Hay was stored in its rooms. Cows, chickens, and pigs made themselves at home. When Louis and Jeanne Cornay arrived in 1975, they had to push out many a stubborn farm animal. "When we were cleaning up, I noticed this really dark, almost black stain, on the eleventh step. Not knowing what it was, we tried to bleach it out, but by the time we had completed the remainder of the restoration, we had given up." Cornay is now glad his attempts to remove the stain were unsuccessful.

A few months after moving in, the Cornays learned of a man who had been born in the house in 1890 and was living in Port Arthur, Texas. They invited him to come and see what he thought of their restoration efforts. "One evening this ninety-year-old man and his wife come tearing up the driveway. He drove himself," says Louis Cornay in amazement. "It was quite a sight. Birds were flying out of the way, dust was blowing, and he came charging up to the house. He was a little bitty fella, barely 5'4", and he says, 'I'm Tumpy Chretien and I've come to see *my* house!'" Cornay interrupts his own story. "Now, Hamilton ("Tumpy") Chretien hasn't been here since the turn of the century, so we bring him in to show him around, and after his first sentence I realize he is going to show us around!"

Louis and Jeanne Cornay followed the crotchety figure to the stairwell, where he proceeded (like the long-dead pirate) to move slowly and deliberately up the steps to the first landing. Stopping abruptly at step number eleven, Tumpy Chretien looked down and announced to the startled Cornays that the bloodstain was still there! The ensuing conversation between Louis Cornay and the elderly Mr. Chretien was a bit contentious.

Responding to Mr. Chretien's identification of the mark, a puzzled Louis Cornay questioned his reference to *The Bloodstain.*

The aged visitor squinted at Louis Cornay and tersely gave a one-syllable reply. "Yes!"

Cornay countered, "How do you know that's a bloodstain?"

The exasperated Tumpy Chretien grabbed Cornay's arm, spitting out, "My granddaddy told me it's a bloodstain."

Unconvinced, Louis pressed on. "Well, how did your granddaddy know it was a bloodstain?"

Stretching his bent frame upwards to look Louis in the eye, Mr. Chretien inhaled a raspy breath, then blew out his final answer. "Because my granddaddy was one of the children in the house the night of the killing, and he told me what Felicité did to save them!"

The episode with the elderly Tumpy Chretien confirmed for Louis Cornay the identity of the ghost who plays devilish tricks to make his point. This is a ghost, believes Cornay, without a sense of humor, a ghost who insists on a little respect.

One of the first signs of a ghostly presence occurred shortly after Cornay opened the home to tours. "One night a bus company asked if they could have a nighttime tour. I allowed them to come and told the story about the guy on the stairs. I sort of laughed up my sleeve." Louis lets out a few staccato "ha-ha-ha" sounds, imitating himself. That evening after making fun of the idea of a ghost in the house, Louis says he began to believe that perhaps the spirit of the slain pirate was indeed hanging around. Cornay was awakened at five o'clock the next morning by the unrelenting bleating of his car horn. He went outside and was about to unplug the wires to disconnect the horn when, instead, for reasons he cannot explain, he reached in the window and passed his hand across the steering wheel. "I ran my hand over it without touching it, sort of like the way you might push someone's hand out of the way, and the horn stopped just like that." Louis snaps his fingers in the air. With the noise gone, Louis went back to bed, but an hour later, the honking resumed. This time, says Cornay, he knew just what to do. "I went outside and ran my hand across the horn pad, pushing the invisible hand away, and the horn stopped."

A few nights later, Cornay relates, he and his wife were hosting a family dinner party and he began talking about the strange occurrences with the car horn. Everyone found the story amusing except for Cornay's cousin, who became quite agitated. Louis firmly told his cousin that the events really did happen exactly as he said. Pounding both hands on the table in outrage, Louis's cousin declared Louis to be crazy—"Ghosts can't make things happen!" Just then the two front doors in the dining room flew open. "They were latched," confirms the present owner, "just like they are latched now."

Several months passed. Louis Cornay put the incidents behind him. As he led another evening tour through rooms decorated with period antiques—mahogany armoires, silk-draped beds, French walnut tables on cabriole legs—Cornay decided to entertain the group with a lighthearted tale of their touchy ghost. He went on at length describing the foolish pirate who fell for Felicité's ruse. Again at precisely five the next morning, the horn on his car began a persistent blaring. Stumbling out of bed, Louis Cornay descended the stairs—making careful note of step eleven—opened the car door, waved his hand over the steering wheel, and the horn stopped.

The practical Mr. Cornay no longer pokes fun at his pirate ghost, preferring to avoid the irritating wakeup call. Louis offers a simple rationale. "The guy was saying don't make fun of me and everything is okay."

Cornay now treads lightly when it comes to supernatural phenomena. "When we first moved into the home, I was skeptical of what you use the word ghost for, and I have decided that instead of ghost, it's energy sources left by people who lived here before. As long as you are respectful of this energy that is in the house, it isn't evil, and it isn't bad or anything—it's just that we're all living here together."

Realizing the marketing potential of this melding of past and present, Chretien Point Plantation hosts "Candlelit Ghost Dinners," where guests are invited to "arrive at dusk, drive through centuries-old oaks dripping with Spanish moss," and as the candles flicker "listen to the legends of Felicité, Hypolite, Jean Lafitte—and 'Robert,'" the name the Cornays have given to the errant pirate who met his end at the hands of a valiant damsel.

Chretien Point has new owners but continues to welcome visitors.

9

Murder, Mystery, and Mayhem at Loyd Hall

A forlorn Union suitor plays the violin on the upper gallery and entertains children in the attic; a cantankerous poltergeist swipes silverware from the table. The spirits of Loyd Hall in Cheneyville stake out their territory, yet former owner Anne Fitzgerald is unfazed. Sitting on the Victorian settee in the front parlor, Mrs. Fitzgerald extends the same cordial welcome to former occupants as she does to overnight guests, who come to savor antebellum life in all its varied forms. Anne Fitzgerald is proud of Loyd Hall's haunted lineup. With her pale-red hair glinting in the sunlight, she declares in an inviting drawl, "We have wonderful ghosts and spirits with us."

Resident tour guide Beulah Davis, a strikingly tall Black woman, bolstered by a proud, ramrod-straight carriage, feels that the hauntings began with William Loyd, the original builder. Standing next to a heavily carved armoire in the master bedroom, the regal Beulah speaks of the red-bearded William as if he has just breezed through the keyhole-framed doorway. "I feel his presence here. He is somewhat of a mysterious-type person."

Anne Fitzgerald supports Beulah's account, noting that William Loyd was accused of being both a Union and a Confederate sympathizer, and wound up "tarred, feathered, and hung from one of the large oaks in the front yard."

In a clipped cadence, Beulah elaborates. "During the Civil War between the Union and the Confederate soldiers, they occupied Loyd Hall at different times. The Unions had taken it as a command post, and the Confederates were camped out in the woodside. William Loyd was caught like a double spy between the two, kind of playing them off, one against the other. I think

Loyd Hall's ghosts seem to stem from the turbulent years of the Civil War.

he's still here today trying to do the same to family members and guests and animals." With unswerving conviction, Beulah expresses her faith in William's supernatural abilities. "He comes in all types of forms at Loyd Hall."

Not surprisingly, Beulah Davis sees nothing strange with the long-deceased William Loyd's own penchant for returning in the phantom shape of a large white dog. If William did indeed spend a lifetime as an expert in subterfuge, then perhaps it is not such a stretch to imagine his soul materializing as a shaggy four-legged creature. Ms. Davis believes that William Loyd's spirit is so persistent because "he really didn't get to finish what he started with this beautiful old house."

Loyd Hall's other ghosts also favor the occasional disguise. "Sometimes it looks like a man and sometimes it looks like a woman; sometimes it may be just a silhouette or a white oval shape." The choice, says the fair-minded Ms. Davis, is arbitrary.

Beulah's first paranormal experiences at this 640-acre working plantation were of the benign variety: muffled footsteps, doors opening and closing, objects moving about. Initially Beulah chalked it up to her imagination. "My parents always told me about visions they had, but until I came to Loyd Hall, I never really truly experienced anything like that." Through the years, as Beulah worked at Loyd Hall, her opinion changed. "In certain rooms when you can see a figure or a shape moving on your side vision, and you know you're the only person that's supposed to be there that's alive, when you kind of catch it, that's when I decided that there was something for real." To the doubters Beulah cautions, "Wait until you have that personal experience and then you decide!"

Floating through the night air thick with the smell of jasmine and gardenia, the first haunting note heard by many guests at Loyd Hall is from a melancholy violin solo by the "Midnight Pied Piper." Surprisingly the tune is not produced by the multitalented William Loyd, a.k.a. "Wily Willie," a.k.a. "The Doggone Trickster." Rather, the ghostly sonata is attributed to one Harry Henry.

Beulah Davis describes Harry as a young Union soldier who

just decided to stay behind and desert his regiment. Anne Fitzgerald indicates there was more than a little incentive for Harry's desertion. "When the Union forces occupied Loyd Hall, Harry became enamored of the attractive niece of the family trapped in the house." According to Mrs. Fitzgerald, when the Union forces pulled out, the lovestruck Harry elected to stay behind and hide in the attic. Wavering between laughter and pity, Anne Fitzgerald recounts the sad twist of fate awaiting the ardent suitor. "Apparently no one informed Grandmother Loyd that Harry was hiding upstairs. Startled at bumping into him, she shot and killed him."

In Beulah's version, Grandmother Loyd and Harry struggle over the gun; the gun goes off and Harry dies. Both Anne and Beulah agree that Harry was buried in a shallow grave under the house, and it is Harry's footsteps that are heard coming down from the attic and crossing onto the balcony, where he commences to play his sad song on the violin. The ghost of hapless Harry strokes his first note at midnight.

When Anne and Frank Fitzgerald first moved into the home that had been renovated by his parents, they, like Teeta Moss and her husband at The Myrtles Plantation in St. Francisville, were concerned about the effect of ghosts and apparitions on their children. Anne explains the situation: "We had three little girls; they were two, five, and nine. It was one thing for them to have visited with their grandmother at Loyd Hall, but quite another for them to live here, go upstairs to bed each evening, and," emphasizes Anne, "I didn't want them to be afraid."

Exercising a mother's prerogative, Anne chose not to talk about ghosts with her daughters, preferring to deal with the haunting issue if, and when, it came up. It arose sooner than expected, and when it did Anne opted for a nonchalant approach.

"I was cooking dinner when I overheard this conversation between the nine year-old and the five-year-old. The nine-year-old said to Melinda: 'What did Harry say today, and what did you and Harry do today?'

"And I'm thinking, *There is no one who works with us here by the name of Harry; we have no relative by the name of Harry; so who is Harry?* Finally I couldn't stand it. I said, 'Girls, who is this Harry we're talking about?'

"They looked at me as if I'd grown two heads and said: 'Mama, Harry is our ghost. He lives on the third floor and plays with us. He's such fun!'"

"Aren't we lucky!" was Anne's quick retort as she went back to stirring the gravy. Her reasoning for not challenging the girls' story was that they were obviously not afraid, and nothing ever occurred to make her uneasy. "Whether it was their active imaginations, or whether Harry had truly joined them, it was a good thing. So we just let them have their fun."

Looking back on her childhood, Melinda Fitzgerald Anderson, Loyd Hall's former manager, has fond memories of her unusual companion. "For years my sister Paige and I had a playmate who was tall, dark, and dressed in a Union uniform. He was like a big brother to us . . . he was the nicest person."

In hindsight, with the Fitzgerald girls grown and with children of their own, Anne does not regret her decision to let her daughters play with a ghost. "It's interesting," reflects Anne. "When we discuss Harry, and I ask them when they first became aware, as children, of the spirit of Harry on the third floor, they'll pause a moment and just say, 'He was always there.' So we take it at that—he just made himself known to them."

Harry continues to make himself known to visitors through his ethereal music, and on rare occasions books himself for a fragmented appearance in the family room. Gesturing to the back of the double parlor, Anne Fitzgerald describes one of these peculiar sightings. "One of the ladies was doing some cleaning in our family room and she felt something. Looking down she saw a pair of shiny black boots and the tip end of a saber as though it was a sword by his side." Anne immediately questioned the woman, seeking a more detailed description of what the "soldier" actually looked like. Shaken, the woman refused to look further and would only repeat over and over: "I just kept cleanin', just kept cleanin'."

Loyd Hall is an equal-opportunity haven for ghosts. Two female spirits also favor the hassle-free accommodations offered by the current owners. Anne Fitzgerald identifies one as a former nanny wearing "a long black dress with draped sleeves, white apron, and a turban on her faceless head." A visiting psychic determined that when the ghost was ready to reveal herself more fully, she would.

Beulah Davis needs no introduction to this ghost. "Her name is Sally. She was a Black nanny that lived in the house with the family but died very mysteriously. They think she might have been poisoned." Beulah swears "Sally" appears during the day in the same room with the boot-and-sword, half-figure apparition of Harry. "I don't know what that room holds for her," admits Beulah, "but on the mantel it is very odd; you cannot keep tall tapered candles standing. We always find 'em lying on the floor. Any other place, any other mantel in the house, they'll stay put."

Anne Fitzgerald says the nanny is also seen in an upstairs bedroom formerly used as a nursery. Today it holds a cradle, and a large four-poster bed with a trio of cloth dolls napping peacefully on an embroidered pillow.

The other known female spirit residing in this circa-1820 Federal-Georgian manor is the victim of unrequited love. Anne Loyd was a niece of William Loyd—a different niece from the one who caused the hapless Harry to desert his regiment. There are no records of what became of niece number one. By contrast, Anne Loyd's death is well documented. Anne was engaged to be married, but her fickle fiancé changed his mind and ran off. The dejected Anne committed suicide by throwing herself out of the third-floor window.

After an unsolicited inspection of the house, the same visiting psychic decreed that the third floor of Loyd Hall contained a high concentration of paranormal activity—not that Beulah Davis or Anne Fitzgerald needed any validation of their ghosts. The psychic also designated the master bedroom on the second floor as the most likely spot to hear footsteps. Anne Fitzgerald allows that this is within the realm of possibilities, as this is the room where William Loyd was placed under house arrest by the Union soldiers before his execution. "I believe that it is him pacing back and forth, not knowing exactly when his demise was going to come, and he was pondering his future."

Undaunted by their tragic fates, the spirits of Loyd Hall rarely brood. Rather, they seem to possess a certain playfulness. Beulah Davis reports that the ghostly antics are just "their small way of letting you know they're here." The tolerant tour guide just wishes they wouldn't move things quite so far. "They change things around. You would at least expect to find it in the same room; instead it's in a totally different part of the house." Snatching knives, forks, and spoons is a favorite prank. "We can set the dining room for lunch or dinner and there's not a time we can sit down that there's not silverware missing. Napkins, glasses, we'll find in other rooms in the house."

Phillip J. Jones, former secretary of the Louisiana Department of Culture, Recreation, and Tourism, lends credence to the stories of moving objects. "There's a wonderful bed and breakfast in the central part of the state called Loyd Hall and we were there having a dinner."

Ms. Davis recalls his visit. "He [Phillip Jones] was sitting at the long dining-room table at the end. They had totally moved his silverware. It was there as he sat down, but as he started to eat his food, he found several pieces missing. He called it to my attention, and that's when I told him, 'I told you the ghosts do exist here.'"

After dinner, the group retired to the front parlor. Former state official Phillip Jones has no easy explanation for the evening's events. "We were listening to the curator [Beulah Davis], who has been in the home giving tours for some twenty years. She said one of the things the ghosts apparently like to do is topple the candlesticks, and as we were sitting there discussing this, one of the candlesticks just came out of its silver holder and fell to the wooden floor." Jones' evaluation of the situation is forthright. "I realized there probably is a little bit of truth to the fact that this home is haunted." The youthful-looking Jones also confesses, "I was a little skeptical at first, you know, but it's a true story. It really is."

Anne Fitzgerald says the tendency of Loyd Hall's ghosts to move objects about is actually an asset. "Our ghosts are wonderful because they do things which save us an embarrassment sometimes. If we have failed to do something or something is out of place, we can always say, 'Well, our ghosts did that, you know—they must have been very active last night.'"

Beulah Davis seconds Anne Fitzgerald's enthusiastic endorsement of the ghosts of Loyd Hall. "We feel like it's a good thing, 'cause we feel like that they're still here in some way, and that they truly watch over this property, I think, and give it an ambiance of its own."

The house itself is a tale of hidden treasure. "One of the real interesting points about this house," declares an amazed Anne Fitzgerald, "is, first of all, my in-laws bought the property without knowing the house was here." Built in the early 1800s, the house was dubbed "Loyd's Folly" due to its mismatched Georgian/Greek Revival architecture and relative isolation on Bayou Boeuf. Piecing together its early history, Anne Fitzgerald refers to one theory that holds that William Loyd was the proverbial black sheep of the prominent Lloyd family of England. The disgraced William was forced to alter his surname, dropping one of the Ls. William Lloyd was born again as William Loyd. Leaving England, he arrived in Tennessee, then headed southward to create a thinly disguised branch of the Lloyd family tree in Louisiana. William Loyd enjoyed a modicum of success until he reverted to some bad habits, playing the "double-agent" game during the Civil War.

After William's hanging at the hands of the Union forces, "Loyd's Folly" was left to William's brother James and remained in the Loyd family until 1871. For the next seventy-one years, Loyd Hall was a victim of bad gambling debts and bad planning. While the fertile soil of the surrounding acreage continued to be tilled and planted with an assortment of crops—cotton, corn, and soybeans—the maintenance of such a large house was beyond the means of the straggling parade of twenty-one unlucky owners. Left exposed to the elements, "Loyd's Folly" fell into such disrepair that it wasn't even listed on legal deeds.

When Anne's in-laws purchased the six hundred plus acres in 1948 to pasture their herd of cattle, no one bothered to tell them there was a house on the property. The senior Fitzgeralds didn't discover they owned an antebellum home, a haunted one at that, until they came out to fence in the herd.

"Two and a half stories, four chimneys, ten rooms [and assorted ghosts]—so overgrown," explains Anne, "you couldn't see it from the road." Another unexpected sweet bonus was 200 pounds of honey dripping from the balcony, courtesy of a thriving colony of bees. Tunneling through years of accumulated debris inside the house, the Fitzgeralds were rewarded by the sight of a suspended staircase fashioned of tiger maple, mahogany, and walnut, intricate ceiling friezes and medallions, hand-carved cypress woodwork, and pine flooring.

Today, visitors to this charming country retreat can enjoy a stay in antique-filled cabins or stroll about a working farm. Horses, chickens, local Catahoula hounds, and Clarence, the donkey, all extend a friendly welcome, a welcome matched only by the resident ghost population.

When asked, Beulah Davis generally recommends nightfall as the most propitious time to bump into one of Loyd Hall's playful spirits. "I feel late evening when the sun is going down, that's probably the time of day they'd have been out working . . . they'd be coming in for the day. So I feel as the shadows falls across the house, late evening, that's when you experience things."

Beulah backs up her tip with one final bit of proof: "I've had the opportunity to stay late, waiting for bed-and-breakfast guests. I'll be sitting in the back parlor—we have a beeper on the door that beeps to let you know when somebody enters the house when we're here by ourself—and I could hear very clear the door open and close. I get up, walk out into the hall expecting to find my guest standing there, and it's nothing."

Nothing but a friendly spirit returning home to Loyd Hall.

Operating under new owners, Loyd Hall continues to welcome guests and ghosts.

In the twenty-first century, Woodland still plays host to visitors and spirits alike.
(Courtesy of Glinda Schafer)

10

The Rising Spirits of Woodland

Few plantations have endured with a tale as turbulent as Woodland. For a time it appeared she would survive only as "The Plantation on a Bottle." Relegated to a label on a whiskey jar, Woodland Plantation on the lower coast below New Orleans teetered on the brink of obscurity. When Foster Creppel came to the rescue of this dilapidated damsel, he uncovered clues pointing to a grand Creole lady—and not-so-subtle hints that the previous occupants were still around.

"Footsteps, the pounding sounded like footsteps," says Foster Creppel. "It was annoying and frustrating at a time when I thought we were doomed forever to live in ruins." To keep a watchful eye on the renovations, Foster camped out in the derelict home. His companions were owls in the attic, alligators in the barrow pit, and a mysterious ghost with a heavy foot.

Woodland Plantation in West Pointe a la Hache was built to last. Floods of biblical proportions, monstrous hurricanes, bootleggers, carpetbaggers, bats and bugs—all left her battered, but unbowed. New owner Foster Creppel is on a mission to restore this proud relic of another era into an appealing country retreat. Paying guests, not ghosts, are Foster's top priority.

Until the Creppels took over in 1997, Woodland Plantation was a forgotten smudge, a blur, along the main drag from New Orleans down to the mouth of the Mississippi River. Louisiana 23 in Plaquemines Parish is a four-lane rumbling chute through the heart of "Sportsman's Paradise." Mammoth oil rigs crisscrossing the horizon provide a thriving habitat for the deep-water denizens of the Gulf of Mexico and a major lure for big-game fishermen. The drone of cars, pickup trucks, and big rigs rolling south is a constant. With Barataria Bay to the right and the low-slung levee of the Mississippi River to the left, favored pit stops for these fishermen, hunters, and oil-rig workers are Port Sulphur, Empire, Buras, Venice, and Pilot Town. Few, if any, feel the tug of the past. Few, if any, note that this stretch of the river was once lined on both banks with more than 360 plantations—Magnolia, Myrtle Grove, Live Oak, Celeste. Today the voices of all but one are silenced. Woodland, the lone holdout, harbors their stories—a ghostly orchestra of shared memories.

Yankee sea captains William M. Johnson and George Bradish staked their claim to the lower coast back in 1780. Together they established Magnolia Plantation. Theirs was a unique living arrangement. The two men, their wives, and children all resided under one roof. As described in *Green Fields: Two Hundred Years of Louisiana Sugarcane,* the conjoined families shared "a large two-story house with gable ends, a large center hall and columns extending through the two stories in front and rear." Magnolia was the first great plantation to greet visitors arriving through the mouth of the Mississippi. It attracted a host of the famous and the infamous, including, of course, the swaggering pirate Jean Lafitte.

For the captains, life was smooth sailing. A few years after installing their families within Magnolia's white-pillared walls, Johnson and Bradish shared the honor of being designated America's first Chief River Pilots. The industrious Johnson also served as the postmaster at Pilot Town (then known as Balize) and justice of the peace for Plaquemines Parish. In short, Johnson and Bradish were gone a lot. Back at Magnolia Plantation, domestic bliss began to unravel. As the children grew, the wives argued incessantly over which of their sons would inherit the grand house and surrounding acreage.

To end the feud, William Johnson, Solomon-like, moved his wife, Sarah Rice, and their children into a new home two miles upriver from Magnolia. Smaller in scale, but with a charming elegance, the residence was known simply as "the Johnson home"; as it gained in stature, it was upgraded to Woodland Plantation.

Capt. William Johnson, now well into his seventies, was ready to retire. Making a final journey to his home state of New York, he left Woodland in the care of his four sons. Two of his sons, George and Bradish Johnson, christened before the family feuds, shared the first and last names of William's former business partner, George Bradish.

The anonymous spirit stalking Woodland Plantation today stays in the shadows. Noisy, yet reticent, he cautiously withholds his true identity. While the Creppels are only the third family of record to own Woodland, potential candidates for "the mysterious ghost in residence" are plentiful.

At the time of the captain's death, Woodland was an 11,000-acre working sugarcane plantation, incorporating a 5,000-square-foot main house, a large sugar mill, a two-story overseer's house, and twenty-four smaller "workers' cabins." It was a small village.

The captain's eldest son, George Washington Johnson, managed the day-to-day operations until his death in 1856. In 1857, Bradish Johnson bought out his brothers' shares in Woodland, becoming the sole owner. Bradish was fond of wearing precision-striped trousers, Prince Albert coats, and black silk hats. A sketch of this proper gentleman would likely include a favorite gold-tipped cane (the better to pound floors with?). If possible, Foster Creppel would have been the first to snatch it away. In Foster's first few months at Woodland, he slept fitfully on a mattress on the first floor. Awakened nightly by fierce pounding overhead, Foster would race up the curved stairwell to be greeted by—silence.

Foster recalls his early tribulations at Woodland, pushing his patience to the edge. "Moving here—everything was in really bad shape. Lots of rats, snakes, rotten wood from the termites. Just the scope of it, I wasn't really ready for it." If the rising spirits of Woodland wanted Foster's undivided attention, they were going to have to take a number and wait their turn.

Years earlier in the spring of 1871, a far more idyllic

picture greeted *Harper's Weekly* reporter Ralph Keeler and artist Alfred Waud. Looking out from the upper deck of the steamboat *Alvin,* they were amazed at the wonders before them: "The river was high, and one actually looked down at the countryside . . . we landed at Woodland, one of the plantations of Mr. Bradish Johnson. Woodland must be his favorite for it is his home while in the South."

Keeler's assessment was accurate. Like his father and brother before him, Bradish was passionately devoted to Woodland—a devotion that may linger still. Although he was in effect an absentee landlord, supervising his Plaquemines Parish holdings from the lofty confines of a Fifth Avenue townhouse in New York City, Bradish returned to Woodland religiously each year for the grinding season (sugarcane harvesting). The dapper and diplomatic Bradish also used his dual citizenship (Yankee and Southern Rebel) to safeguard his ancestral home during the Civil War. He persuaded the U.S. provost marshal to set up headquarters at Woodland. The Federal troops left the Southern residence of the Yankee businessman virtually unscathed.

Spared from the destruction and raids suffered by many neighboring plantations, Woodland enjoyed its greatest period of prosperity after the war.

Stepping off the gangplank of the riverboat, artist Alfred Waud grabbed his sketchpad, capturing late-nineteenth-century Woodland at its peak. Golden stalks of sugarcane rippled in the fields; a carriage, drawn by a pair of dappled grays, bore three lovely ladies, parasols raised to protect their delicate skin from the sun; Woodland with its red-tiled roof and windows open to catch the breeze off the river glimmered like a jewel of Southern hospitality. Waud's captivating sketch of Woodland first appeared in the weekly tabloid *Every Saturday* and set off a chain of events still evident at Woodland today.

Lithographers Nathaniel Currier and James Merritt Ives catapulted Woodland into the limelight when they appropriated Waud's charming sketch for their popular *Homes Across the Country* series. Like early travel posters, the fashionable prints featured a representative home from each region of the country. Currier and Ives did a little revamping of the original Waud sketch, reversing it and tossing in some embellishments of their own like a steamboat in the foreground puffing upriver, and another horse-drawn buggy. They even gussied up the plain box columns in the front with ornate Corinthian capitals. The addition of a half-dozen hoop-skirted ladies, escorted by equally elegant gentlemen, strolling arm in arm about the grounds conveyed the message that life along the Mississippi was an endless round of leisurely teas and parties. Woodland Plantation in West Pointe a la Hache became the poster child for the Grand Old South. This image of Woodland's opulent lifestyle caught the marketing eye of the Southern Comfort Corporation.

In the 1880s a Bourbon Street bartender, M. W. Herron, concocted his own masterpiece just a few miles upriver in New Orleans. He named his full-bodied marvel with a hint of sweetness "Southern Comfort," serving the potent drink directly from a whiskey barrel. As with every successful business enterprise, it's all in the packaging, and by 1934 the Southern Comfort Corporation was on the lookout for the perfect picture for their new label to celebrate the end of Prohibition. The Currier and Ives print of Woodland Plantation soon graced every bottle of "Southern Comfort."

In a bizarre twist, just as the label lured millions to savor the smooth spirits of the new "Grand Old Drink of the South," Woodland was drowning in a swirling tide of misfortune. Bradish Johnson died in 1897 and Woodland was sold to a Theodore Starks Wilkinson. Wilkinson, also the owner of Myrtle Grove Plantation, downgraded Woodland to a hunting lodge. Campaigning unsuccessfully for governor of Louisiana, the overextended Wilkinson amassed a $19,000 debt. He forked over Woodland to his brother Horace as repayment on a loan.

The 1920s saw Prohibition etch a new face on the American landscape. Now virtually abandoned, Woodland, with her prime location near the mouth of the Mississippi River, was a favorite haven for bootleggers. They camped out in the great upper hall, where the dormer windows, front and back, provided perfect lookouts. When federal agents arrived on the scene, they watched in frustration as the alert bootleggers tossed the evidence into the river.

By the 1940s, a jungle of weeds enveloped the main house, the sugar mill receded into the forest, and vandals made off with whatever they could carry. Her 11,000 acres were parceled and sold off. The ghosts of Woodland's glory days settled in for a long sleep.

Occasionally an ambitious reporter would file a story: "Woodland Plantation: A Shadow of What It Used to Be"; "Woodland Plantation: Life on the Mississippi"; "Plantation in Peril." The articles stirred little interest. Current residents of the lower coast were intent on pursuing oil and mineral rights. Plantations were a blip in the past. And connoisseurs savoring their smooth Southern Comfort cocktails had no inkling that the mysterious plantation appearing on the bottle actually existed. Like Cinderella in tatters, Woodland lost her invitation to the ball.

Over the years, attempts were made to document this last surviving relic of Plaquemines Parish. In 1997 Tulane University professor of architecture Eugene Cizek, with a grant from the Louisiana Department of Culture, Recreation, and Tourism, surveyed the crumbling buildings. Woodland's thirteen heirs, descendants of Horace Wilkinson, were embroiled in a bitter battle of legal title and rights. Under a court-ordered settlement, the Plaquemines Parish Sheriff's Office auctioned Woodland to the highest bidder. The winning bidders, Foster Creppel and his parents, Jacques and Claire, walked away with a piece of Louisiana history.

Renovating Woodland was like prying open a damaged time capsule. Each shovelful of dirt removed, each sagging floorboard uncovered, each rotten timber, threw up much in the way of discouragement. But like avid treasure hunters, the Creppels also rejoiced when Woodland gave up one of her hoarded secrets.

Evidence of William Johnson's haste to separate the feuding

wives at Magnolia Plantation is revealed in the construction of Woodland. Interior walls are at odds with the exterior. The exterior is square and true: front and back views boast seven matching cypress columns, five matching dormer windows, and a broad gallery. Foster Creppel also points to "the two large chimneys on both ends of the house," which "act as anchors" for the entire structure. Once the debris was removed, the inside of Woodland revealed a surprisingly helter-skelter floor plan. One window on the first floor is covered and bisected by an interior wall, while another wall slants crookedly to avoid cutting off a second window. Foster Creppel is left to speculate whether William or Sarah was responsible for changing their minds after the house was built, or if they were just in too much of a hurry to get out of Magnolia and quickly threw together some plans.

These elusive tidbits have allowed the Creppels to see the plantation through the eyes of those who knew her best: William and Sarah Johnson and their sons. Knocking down bee, wasp, and termite nests, the Creppels found a broken fragment of a blue stenciled border under the eaves of a second-floor bedroom. Fourteen months of intensive labor later, this same room is proudly rewrapped with a replica blue-ribboned border. Filling in the gaps in the curved mahogany balustrade of the stairway was like connecting the dots to the past. Now a host of ghostly hands can continue their slow descent to the parlor.

With renovations complete, the foot-pounding ghost has ceased his stomp-dance overhead. Perhaps it was just the long-dormant spirit of Captain Johnson, unaccustomed to the racket of construction, or his proper son Bradish, cane in hand, demanding peace and quiet.

As he pokes and prods, unearthing Woodland's multilayered history, Foster Creppel finds cryptic messages in shards of pottery, broken bottles, and rusting tools. The grounds of Woodland are a giant archeological dig—the mysteries of the overseer's cabin and the old sugar mill await future exploration.

Foster took a little detour in 1999, unable to resist the lure of another historic building filled to the rafters with life's joys and sorrows. An 1880s country Gothic-style chapel was slated for demolition. The roof was gone, the floorboards were rotten, and the walls in the apartment behind the altar were marred with satanic symbols and pentagrams. But the price was right. All Foster Creppel had to do was move it fourteen miles upriver to Woodland. Undeterred, this diehard preservationist had St. Patrick's Church cut in half and loaded onto two flatbed trucks. At Woodland the deconsecrated chapel was born again as a restaurant aptly named "The Spirits of Woodland." Arched stained-glass windows cast a rainbow of pastel colors over the polished hardwood floors. The former altar is now a bar, where patrons receive their choice of libations in lieu of sermons.

Ghosts of former parishioners drawn to the old parish church of St. Patrick must make a few adjustments. Forgoing the traditional seating in church pews, the spectral congregation must sit in a circle around the new dining-room configuration. They have, at least for now, let the mortal diners enjoy their meals in relative peace.

Combined, the reincarnation of Woodland Plantation as a country inn and the transformation of a rural church to a restaurant preserve a timeless bond with the families who once populated the lower coast below New Orleans.

11

A Capitol Ghost

Louisiana's phantoms have a penchant for plantations; favoring spacious digs, they roam in spectral splendor. One capricious soul upped the ante, electing to haunt a medieval fortress that glows at sunset, eerily reminiscent of Count Dracula's beloved castle in Transylvania.

The Old State Capitol in Baton Rouge looms high on a bluff overlooking the murky Mississippi. Its haphazard Gothic-Victorian architecture harks back to the warring ways of feudal lords, vassals, and serfs. Twin turreted towers, crenellated upper battlements, a stained-glass dome festooned with a disorienting array of cobalt-blue, topaz-gold, and blood-red patches—all cast a hypnotic spell. Given Louisiana's propensity for political squabbles and legislative wrangling, the antiquated structure seems well suited, in form and function, to its intended purpose as the seat of state government. The ghost within delights in taunting the staff. Leaving a trail of dusty footprints, he darts through hallowed halls, zipping up and down the spiral staircase. Triggering alarms, he swipes small objects at random. He's known as Pierre, "The Keeper of the Castle." Herein lies the tale of a capitol ghost, the story of a man so obsessed with missing out on his appointed mission in life that he sent his spirit to fill in for him—the ultimate *voter in absentia*.

Pierre Couvillon served as a member of the Louisiana House of Representatives and the Senate from 1834 to 1851. Described in biographical records as a "gargantuan" man standing more than six feet tall with "a body well proportioned to that height," he relied on his powerful, domineering physical attributes to

High on a bluff, the Old State Capitol looms over the murky Mississippi River.

intimidate his opponents. Like all good politicians, Pierre also possessed a flip side, fluidly switching on his "irresistible personality" and "entrancing storytelling ability" to endear himself to family, friends, and constituents. This firebrand with the dual personality vehemently opposed the corrupt banking practices of the day, lobbying vigorously, according to family legends, to protect the interests of the common man.

Accounts differ on the details of Pierre's death and his ensuing haunted appearances at the Old State Capitol. One version has him succumbing to a heart attack in the heat of a passionate speech against corruption during the 1852 legislative session. His inopportune but dramatic demise is the primary reason officials suspect his spirit of causing the disturbances in the building. Phillip J. Jones, former secretary of the Louisiana Department of Culture, Recreation, and Tourism, has heard this bit of folklore but states that history does not support this colorful account. "He [Pierre] didn't die in the Old State Capitol, although he did actually have a tremendous fit. He was at his home in Avoyelles Parish and had a heart attack and died."

Historic records verify that two months prior to the start of the 1852 session, while Pierre was at home, he learned that some of his fellow legislators were eliciting financial favors from the banking establishment (at taxpayers' expense); he exploded over their outrageous conduct.

Pierre was laid to rest in Mansura Catholic Cemetery, leaving behind a wife, ten children, and a seat in the Louisiana State Senate. In a 1996 official press release headlined "Gen. Pierre Couvillon's Ghost Believed to Reside at Old State Capitol," former Louisiana State Archives Assistant Director Lewis Morris suggests that Pierre's obsession with truth and justice may be the reason his spirit made the long journey from his home in Avoyelles Parish back to Baton Rouge. "He was a powerful orator, and he often spoke out against those who used their office and influence to enrich themselves at the expense of those less fortunate." Morris adds, "It was his sincerity for the ordinary man that played a role in his untimely death."

It is also understandable why Pierre's ghost is a tad put out. Having endured the hassle of returning from the dead and trekking back to the capitol building to keep a vigilant eye on his fellow lawmakers, he has a hard time finding them at work. Some may smile ruefully, saying nothing has changed. However, in Pierre's case, the issue is not one of do-nothing politics, but of logistics. Although he has stoically witnessed a litany of dramatic developments at the capitol during his ghostly tenure, including the tragic vote to secede from the Union in 1861 and the seizure of the capitol by Yankee forces in 1862, Pierre struggles to keep up. The ghostly lawmaker had just marked his first decade of haunting his former cronies, when the Union troops put a torch to the state capitol.

For twenty years after the fire (1862-82), the blackened hulk of the capitol building sat lifeless; Louisiana's government went into exile, moving in a gypsy caravan from Baton Rouge to Opelousas to Shreveport to New Orleans. Despite Pierre's pressing need to haunt halls of the old state capitol building, many citizens favored demolition, expressing disdain for the dilapidated structure. Others sought to preserve the historic building and return the capital to Baton Rouge. Samuel Langhorne Clemens (better known as Mark Twain) sided with the former. Clemens spied "this little sham castle" on his epic 1882 journey downriver. Penning his distaste for its awkward medieval appearance, the river pilot-turned-commentator wrote in *Life on the Mississippi:* "It is pathetic enough that a whitewashed castle, with turrets and things . . . should ever have been built in this otherwise honorable place . . . but it is even more pathetic to see this architectural falsehood undergoing restoration and perpetualization in our day, when it would have been so easy to let dynamite finish what a charitable fire began."

Perhaps Pierre's spectral hand, raised aloft, *was* counted during the tally of *yeas* and *nays* (voting from beyond the grave, cynics claim, is also a time-honored tradition in Louisiana politics), for eventually, after a good deal of wrangling, the preservationists won. Architect William Freret began restoration work on the "Castle" in 1882 and the legislators returned to Baton Rouge under Pierre's watchful eye.

But by 1932, Louisiana lawmakers decided the castle's nooks and crannies were simply two crowded; they needed more modern accommodations and voted to move their offices to a new, larger Art Deco structure down the road. This time poor phantom Pierre was left entirely in the lurch. Spirits of the dead do not necessarily return to haunt with all their faculties intact and "can't always go where they want to." Pierre's ghost was dismayed to find he had once again lost track of the lawmakers.

For the next six decades the architectural oddity limped along as a meeting space for various civic and cultural groups. The worn-out specter of Pierre faded with the much-maligned "Castle."

Yet the landmark "Castle" was not without supporters. In 1981, a meticulous thirteen-year, $9.25 million restoration was launched. And in 1994 Pierre's beloved capitol building reopened its hand-hewn cypress doors as Louisiana's Center for Political and Governmental History. Today the museum's gleaming interior belies 150 years of scandal, intrigue, impeachment, the occasional fistfight on the floor, and a long line of combative governors topped by the "Kingfish," Huey Long. At its grand opening, some reviewers raved that the refurbished "Castle" took on a "wedding-cake perfect" persona.

All that spit and polish woke the dormant Pierre. Perplexed at the new state of affairs, he vents his frustration on the staff at the "new" Old State Capitol Museum. Mary Louise Prudhomme, former director of the complex, says their first hint of a phantom visitor came from a student worker in the museum's gift shop. "She said the door would open and close all by itself—we have these large heavy doors that don't exactly swing in the breeze." Ms. Prudhomme takes the direct approach; she's a Southern-to-the-core, face-things-head-on, *Steel Magnolia* woman. A tailored cherry-red suit sets off her clipped dark-brown hair. "Now, no one," she declares emphatically, "was really frightened. They just knew it was kind of strange. As more of the employees became involved—

coming to me and discussing things that happened to them personally—we began to sense that perhaps we did have ghost."

Former security guard/guide John Hoover has no doubt that the ghostly campaign of the "lawmaker extraordinaire" is back in high gear. The gun and holster slung on Hoover's hip seem an odd fit for the kindly grandfather figure with his cap of thick, snow-white hair, but he takes his job seriously. Hoover cleverly turns the pesky Pierre's manifestations to his advantage, using tales of the capitol ghost to keep groups of visiting schoolchildren in line. "I tell the kids that something happened one night that changed my ideas about whether we had a ghost in the building or not."

John takes center stage in the expansive Senate Chamber on the second floor. Sunlight streams through the stained-glass Gothic windows, casting a crazy-quilt mosaic over the oak-planked floor. A group of fourth graders sits cross-legged in a lopsided semicircle at John's feet. Security cameras mounted high on brackets scan the room. John Hoover reminds his captive audience that they are under constant surveillance. "I point out that we have forty security cameras in this building and underneath the cameras is a little white box we call a motion detector." John follows this with a little a demonstration. "I'll have a student or maybe one of the teachers walk towards the motion detector that's behind us here, so they can see a little red light come on. I explain to them that the light not only lights up here at that box, but it also lights up downstairs at the main security board."

Now that John has laid out the parameters for the defense of the building from the invasion of any intruders (mortal or otherwise), he sets the scene for the night in question. The Capitol Museum is open during the day to tour groups and individuals; at night its vaulted rooms, chambers, and gallery spaces are rented out for a variety of functions from wedding receptions to fundraisers. When the building is not in use, John tells the squirming kids, the sophisticated monitoring system is supervised by a single guard stationed in front of the security board on the first floor.

At this juncture in his story, John gets down to the scary details: It is 10:30 P.M. Former night security guard Wanda Lee Porter is on duty and has relieved the day guard. The motion detector under camera #22 lights up on the security board. Camera #22 is positioned on the first floor, aimed at "The Old Governor's Mansion Collection." The display consists of three rooms: a dining room and two bedrooms. All are decorated with period furniture from past governors. As the light blinks on the board, security guard Porter immediately punches up camera #22 on the big screen so she can scan one of the bedrooms and look at what has set off the motion detector. She sees nothing. She gets on the phone to check in with the guard she has relieved from the day shift. She asks him if he left "anyone in the building" without telling her. His unequivocal response is "No, indeed no."

Wanda punches up camera #22 again, rescanning the bedroom. "I looked high and I looked low—still nobody." The motion detector under camera #22 continues its flashing. Checking the screen again, she is still unable to pinpoint the source of the problem. Alone and nervous, Wanda tries to talk herself through it. "Somethin' wrong here . . . maybe I ought to go down and look." Hoping whatever it is will just go away, Wanda pushes her chair back, tightens the belt around her small waist, unhooks the key to the bedroom, and makes a final sweep with the camera. "I waited a little minute to see if I was going to see anything." To Wanda's relief, the motion detector stops its warning signal in the bedroom, but before she can exhale in gratitude, another detector flashes on in the adjoining room. "It came on in the dining room. I was thinkin', *Oh Lord, something wrong here.* So I brought the camera direct to that table—still didn't see nothin'." The pitch of Wanda's voice rises as she remembers her attempts to catch the invisible intruder.

John praises Wanda's next move. "She's brave. She gets her flashlight, goes down the hallway, unlocks the door [to the Governor's Mansion display], and turns the lights on."

Wanda's cautious search reveals no evidence of the

mysterious trespasser. "I looked all up under the bed; I looked behind the curtains." As she is about to leave, Wanda notices something peculiar. "I looked over towards the bed. The covers looked a little cranky." ("Cranky" is Wanda's wonderfully descriptive colloquialism for something messy or out of place.) Racing through Wanda's mind is the panicky notion that *Oh Lord, somebody or something's been here*. Backtracking, Wanda locks the doors and hurries back to the main security station to "start over from scratch."

Seated in the relative safety of her office, Wanda takes a few moments to reassess what's happened. The motion detector has stopped blinking, and she considers that maybe it has all just been a fluke; maybe the cleanup crew accidentally bumped into the bed and neglected to straighten the covers. But Wanda's comfort zone is rocked when the ghostly hijinks hit auto rewind. Now the motion detector under camera #21 kicks on. Wanda flips the video from camera #21 onto the big screen—nothing out of the ordinary appears. Then like a string of Christmas twinkle lights, the motion detectors in the hallway are set off in eerie progression, as if someone or *something* is passing by. Wanda is fearful. *Oooh, whatever it is, it's coming this way*. Staring intently at the camera monitors, Wanda fervently prays for a logical explanation for the bizarre phenomenon. Nothing. Wanda knows she should be seeing something, anything, to explain the rippling lights on the motion detector panel.

The triggering of the motion detectors comes to an abrupt halt, indicating "it" has paused at the bottom of the great cast-iron staircase in the rotunda. "By the time the lights stop again at the stairs, I stick my head out and peep." Rhetorically Wanda questions, *Now, I'm assuming that it went upstairs, right?*

Wanda's worst fears are confirmed when she looks over her shoulder at the security board. The motion detector light under camera #30 flashes red, announcing that there is activity in the Senate Chamber on the second floor.

As the sole guard on duty, Wanda knows she must follow through. Carefully she winds her way up the imposing staircase.

At the top of the great rotunda, facing the front of the building, is the hallowed Senate Chamber. Garbed in her security uniform of dark brown trousers and white shirt, the solitary figure of Wanda Lee Porter approaches the massive oak doors. Wanda hesitantly places her hand on the silver door handle embossed with the state seal. She squeezes the lever, yanking the door open. Plunging in, she reaches over and quickly flips on the lights. The peaked roof and elaborate cypress millwork are illuminated by replicas of 1880s restorer William Freret's original gas chandeliers. The only furniture in the cavernous room is a small desk surrounded by a wooden guardrail, hugging the far right-hand corner. Over the desk hangs a portrait of a former senator, the Honorable Pierre Couvillon.

It takes a few seconds for Wanda to process the evidence before her. The chamber has been recently occupied. A dusty trail mars the gleaming surface of the polished floor. "I see these footprints as if somebody had walked from across the room towards the desk." Wanda's sole thought is, *Oh my God, they got a ghost in here.* Shaken, she rushes out, spiraling down the staircase, and grabs for the nearest phone. Wanda calls another guard to let him know "something is very wrong." Her second call is to former director Mary Louise Prudhomme to inform her that "something is in this building, and I don't know what it is . . . *whatever* it is, I'm going to get out of here!" Wanda's voice picks up pace as she catapults through the recital of events. Former director Prudhomme asks Wanda to wait a minute, calm down, and stay there; she is on her way and wants Wanda to show her and explain what has happened. Wanda raises her eyebrows, questioning if any sane person would sit still in her position. Fortunately for Wanda, the backup security guard arrives for moral and physical support. The conversation between the two guards borders on comic relief given the evening's surreal content.

After listening to Wanda describe the blinking lights and the mysterious footprints, the backup guard asks her, "What do you think it is?"

Wanda bats the question right back. "What *you* think it is?"

Both guards are skittish, as neither wants to be the first to acknowledge the presence of a ghost. Wanda sums up their brief stalemate. "I didn't want him to be thinkin' I was crazy, and he didn't want me to think he was thinkin' I was crazy."

Believing she has nothing more to lose when he asks a second time, Wanda blurts out: "A ghost, what else?" Shaking off goose bumps, she admits, "I never seen that like in my life." In a whispered aside she tacks on, "It really frightened me a whole lot. It really did!"

John Hoover winds up his story to the children by stating that security guard Porter must also write up a report on the incident, and the report is sent on to the secretary of state, Fox McKeithen. "A man, an alleged expert," says John with a small smirk, "is sent to check out the building. He goes up in the attic, spends about an hour and a half. He comes down and gives us a typewritten report that he has found evidence that *something* exists in the attic of the Senate."

John Hoover ends his tale to the visiting schoolchildren by telling them two things: "One thing I asked you to do when you first came in is not too make too much noise, because I never want you to wake Pierre during the daytime when I'm here, and second, I can't get Ms. Porter to work the night shift anymore." John says his tale usually works pretty well. The children are quiet for the remainder of the tour and he often spots them looking over their shoulders at the motion detectors.

David Bonaventure, former maintenance supervisor for the Old State Capitol Museum, is not amused by these stories, or by the antics of the ghostly Pierre. When the capitol building reopened its doors as a museum in 1994, there was a rush of tourists and researchers eager to check out the new Center for Political and Governmental History. Most visitors gazed in awe at the grand restoration honored by the American Institute of Architects. The impact of checkerboard black-and-white marble floors, salmon-colored walls, and sage-green cast-iron fretwork, all crowned by the psychedelic swirl of a stained-glass dome in the rotunda, was mesmerizing. But David Bonaventure saw not what was in place but what was missing. "It was the crown," David points out. "It disappeared right after we opened."

The crown David refers to is not an adornment for the head of a king or queen, but rather a wide circular gold rim, part of the restored lights outside the Senate Chamber on the second floor. Two factors made this disappearance stand out: one, the missing "crown" was a rather mundane architectural element, not intrinsically valuable, and two, in order for a thief to have absconded with the gold banding, he would have needed a ladder to reach it—or have the ability to levitate some twenty feet above the floor. Former director Prudhomme says David prefaced his report to her about the missing gold crown with "I know you're going to think I'm crazy but . . ." Prudhomme states unequivocally that David Bonaventure is "a very practical guy, not given to jumping to supernatural conclusions."

For David, the most unsettling part about the string of missing objects was not their disappearance, but rather their reappearance. Six months after the gold rim vanished, it reappeared in its appointed place gracing the top of the light.

Leaning his five-foot-ten, tightly toned frame against the cinder-gray walls in the bowels of the building's basement, this maintenance specialist would also love to get his hands on Pierre's hidden cache of misappropriated tools. Perhaps he is just tidying up, but the persnickety Pierre has a proclivity for pliers. By last count David Bonaventure has "lost" fifteen pairs. "I'll put them down and when I turn around they're gone." Keeping up with the sticky-fingered Pierre's endless pranks is a full-time job, and David would just as soon send out for the nearest ghost buster. On Pierre's last foray into the supervisor's domain, David finally had a witness to the kleptomaniac tendencies of the capitol ghost.

A benefit was planned in the Senate Chamber for the Woman's Hospital of Baton Rouge. A key component of the decorations was an expensive painting arriving in its own custom crate. Maintenance worker Chris Beard lent a helping hand. Together Chris and David unloaded the crate. "It had instructions on top of the crate on how to open it and get the painting out. Chris and I read the instructions. It had a series of screws you first had to remove from the top; they were circled in black ink, like marks-a-lot. We got a drill and removed every one of those top screws, put all the screws on the table behind us, took the top off, removed the portrait from the crate, sat the painting against the wall, put the top back on the crate, grabbed the screws, and started screwing them back in." With a slight hesitation in his voice David adds, "we only had half of them. The rest of the screws were gone." David quickly rattles off the facts: "No one entered the room. It was just me and Chris. We looked for them everywhere for about five minutes—couldn't find them."

Not one to dwell on mysteries, David and his fellow worker went next door to his office, sat down to hash out a few more logistics for the evening's event, then returned to the storage room to get the painting. The first thing David and Chris noticed when they opened the locked door to the storage room were the missing screws lined up, like a regiment of soldiers ready for inspection. "They were laying on top of the table," states Bonaventure. "I have no idea what happened. All I know is that the screws showed up. Nobody could get in the room while we were in there or while we were gone." When asked for his opinion on supernatural phenomena, David scrunches up his pale face, the tips of his short mustache brushing his cheeks, and allows that "I went from a firm believer in not believing to—I'll believe just about anything now."

The down-to-earth Bonaventure is embarrassed over the notoriety such episodes have generated. His struggle to keep up with the packrat habits of Pierre was featured in a 1997 Baton Rouge newspaper article. During an interview for *The Haunting of Louisiana* television documentary, the camera-shy, thirty-something maintenance supervisor appears resigned to the constant ribbing by his friends over his scuffles with the capitol ghost.

On the other hand, former director Prudhomme has embraced the idea of a haunted building. The new marketing brochure features the capitol building basking under a purple night sky. An illuminated ruby-red glass window over the fortresslike front door beckons all those who dare to enter. The flip side of the brochure lists pertinent information about the museum, its exhibits and events, and in bold red, all caps, a single-line reminder: "DON'T FORGET ABOUT PIERRE—OUR GHOST." Prudhomme's rationale for placing Pierre prominently on the museum's brochure is: "People are interested in something beyond what's here today. They want to believe there *is* something for us to look forward to; certainly I think all of us do. So because of that, I believe it's a good marketing tool, and it happens to reach a lot of people."

At the same time, Prudhomme concedes not everyone agrees that hyping a ghost is good for the image. "We have had some negative reaction from certain organizations that do not feel that it is appropriate for us as a museum, or a center for political history, or a state facility, to be, quote unquote, 'advertising that perhaps there could be a ghost in the old state capitol.'" Says Mary Louis Prudhomme with a pragmatic shrug of her narrow shoulders, "That's something you deal with, with almost everything you do. . . . It's had mixed reviews."

Shoring up her decision to promote Pierre, former director Prudhomme balances the negative with the positive: "Pierre [the ghost] has taken on a life of his own. He certainly was a respected person during his lifetime, so we respect him here. We try to be good to everybody—just in case. Right?"

The diminutive ghost at the Lafitte Guest House often appears crying.

12

Little Girl Lost

Like Alice in Wonderland, the spirit of a young girl is trapped in the looking glass at the Lafitte Guest House. Overlooking Lafitte's Blacksmith Shop and Bar, this intimate corner hotel stands in quiet contrast to its bawdy neighbor. At the bar couples laugh and drink. Next door on the second-floor landing, a little girl cries. Her name is Marie. In the 1850s, a petite five-year-old lived with her family in this richly appointed four-story home. Marie has never left.

Downstairs in the Victorian parlor, wearing all the trappings of a nineteenth-century English gentleman—top hat, cape, walking cane, pocket watch—Tom Duran spins a poignant rendition of "Little Girl Lost." Duran, a former curator at London's House of Detention Prison Museum who now makes a living conducting historic tours, has an affinity for apparitions. While leading his New Orleans Ghost Tour through the French Quarter, he weaves the sad tale of a confused child who cannot seem to find her way out. Caught in a time warp, the small female ghost repeatedly exits a bedroom, walks down the hall, and passes through a gilt-framed, five-foot mirror mounted at the far end of the second-floor landing.

In his clipped British accent, Tom Duran recounts what happens after guests check in: "People walk up the stairs and turn towards the mirror. They see behind them the reflection of a little girl. She's normally crying and when she appears, she appears as real as you or I. Of course, what people do is turn around to have a look at this crying girl, but there's nothing there. They turn back and look at the mirror and there's nothing there either. She has simply disappeared. And that happens time and time again."

As proof, Duran whips out a photograph. The enlargement captures a pale form curling around a doorway. Duran says Marie has been caught on camera at least four times since 1960. He confirms that she is always seen leaving the same room. "In the photographs that I've taken on my tour, she's floating out of what is today room 22. Rooms 21 and 22 were the former children's rooms," explains Duran. "In earlier times the children slept to the front and the adults slept to the back."

Duran thinks the waiflike ghost he calls Marie may be the daughter of the original owners, Paul Joseph Gleises and his wife, Marie Odalie Ducayet. Paul Gleises was a local businessman. Marie Odalie was a daughter of the prominent Ducayet family; the Ducayets owned a grand plantation-style home on the banks of Bayou St. John, just outside New Orleans.

When Paul and Marie Gleises moved into their new home on then-fashionable Bourbon Street, it boasted a traditional double parlor and dining room on the first level and six bedrooms spread over the second and third floors. The large attached wing at the rear of the home had rooms for the servants, a kitchen, carriage house, stable, and coal house.

Based on research by the hotel's former hosts and managers, Andrew Crocchiolo and Edward Doré, there were six Gleises-Ducayet children, but only three survived to adulthood. Crocchiolo and Doré also discovered that shortly before the Civil War, Paul Gleises transferred the deed to the house to his wife. Perhaps anticipating the ravages of war that were soon to befall the South, the couple packed up the remaining children, moving first to Philadelphia, then settling in New York. Paul Gleises died in 1898 at the age of seventy-eight. The widow Marie lived to the age of ninety. Little is known of what happened to the children.

From 1866 to the late 1960s, the house survived an assortment of owners until it was rescued by Crocchiolo and Doré, who transformed the once-elegant Gleises home into a charming hotel.

Researcher Tom Duran still has a dilemma. "The problem I'm having investigating this haunting is that I've traced back on the family records, and I've discovered a strange fact about this household. . . . There were five little girls who lived here. They were all called Marie. They all died before their fifth birthday." Duran says several of the girls probably died during the yellow-fever epidemics that swept through the city in the summer of 1853 and again in 1854. New Orleans' cemeteries are dotted with the tear-stained tombs of infants and small children, who succumbed to a grim shopping list of life-threatening diseases—cholera, tuberculosis, pneumonia, even the common cold.

Duran believes that the miniature apparition in the mirror is one of the little Maries who never got to blow out the fifth candle on her birthday cake. But at the moment, he has more questions than answers: Is the tiny ghost one of Marie Ducayet Gleises' daughters who died in infancy? Or is she one of the other Maries who lived in the house in later years? What spell in the mirror lures the small spirit and holds her captive? The English ghost buster swears, "I'll get to the bottom of it one day!"

Hauntings induce peculiar reactions. Just as in Lewis Carroll's magical tale of *Alice in Wonderland*, odd things happened to the young actress who was recreating the role of the diminutive ghost during the filming of *The Haunting of Louisiana*.

With her finely chiseled features, fawn complexion, dark hair, and luminous eyes, a local five-year-old was perfectly cast as the lost Creole child, Marie. The television documentary's director of photography, Oak Lea, was looking forward to working with the diminutive and lively Cedar GrayHawk-Perkins; Oak had served as one of the elders at Cedar's naming ceremony. As the daughter of Annette, a member of the Sault Ste. Marie band of Chippewa, and GrayHawk, a tribal member of the Houmas of Louisiana, young Cedar had already participated in numerous Native American ceremonial activities and loved being in front of the camera. Both of Cedar's parents were there for the taping of the ghost sequence at the Lafitte Guest House.

As the crew worked on lighting on the second floor, the young actress happily laughed and played in the parlor. When grip Heather Genter came downstairs to inform Cedar and her parents they were ready to start, the carefree child lost her smile. The scene called for the actress to slowly walk past the doorway of room 22 and approach the mirror. Director Lea was positioned on the steps over the second-floor landing near the haunted looking glass. When he cued Cedar to start walking, she refused to budge. Lea stopped tape and knelt before the distraught child; tears pooled in her brown eyes, dribbled down her cheeks, and fell in tiny spatters onto her pink nightgown. Each attempted take ended with the same disastrous results: Cedar would tentatively place one bare foot forward in the carpeted hallway, look at the mirror looming over her—and freeze. The normally animated child would not speak, but only stare at the mirror and cry.

The precarious situation was partially resolved by placing Cedar's parents at either end of the hall. Leaving the comforting arms of her father, eyes downcast to avoid the dreaded mirror, Cedar aimed for the outstretched arms of her mother, waiting just beyond the frame of the camera. As soon as the take was over and she was free of the mirror's spell, the frightened actress reemerged as a bubbling little girl.

Did Cedar see something in the mirror none of the adults present could discern? Raised by parents with traditional tribal beliefs, Cedar has been taught since birth that all life is sacred; death is part of the cycle of life. Annette says this is not the first time her young daughter has "seen" something others could not.

13

The Ghostly Decorator

Not all of the New Orleans French Quarter's spirits are intent on evil. Surveying the Victorian elegance of the double parlor in the Lanaux Mansion, Ruth Bodenheimer is well pleased with the decorating flair of her ghostly housemate. "Mr. Charles Andrew Johnson built this glorious house in 1879. He was a wonderful gentleman and a practicing attorney. . . . There was not a Mrs. Johnson so he did all this decorating himself."

Ruth's generous compliment is not totally accurate, as she neglects to take a bow for her own considerable efforts. The ongoing restoration of this Renaissance-Revival townhouse on Esplanade Avenue at the edge of the French Quarter is an interesting collaboration combining some "spirited suggestions" from a fastidious ghost and lots of "implementation" from its mortal owner.

Insisting on giving full credit to the phantom Mr. Johnson, Ruth Bodenheimer reiterates, "It's always his guiding hand. I always say he is my partner in caring for the house, because he knows exactly what I'm doing." The novelty of having a personal decorator on call is surpassed only by the realization that these tasteful tidbits arrive via a spiritual hotline from the netherworld.

Despite their close-working relationship, Ruth Bodenheimer maintains a respectful formality with Mr. Johnson, never lapsing into the more casual mode of addressing her gentleman ghost as Charles or Charlie. Sitting down on the plum-colored settee, she explains how it works. "He's instrumental if I have a major project, especially if it's a costly one. I'll have little private chats with him."

Ruth Bodenheimer at the Lanaux Mansion with a portrait of the original owner.

Mr. Johnson's black-velvet top hat rests on a small marble-topped tea table, as if he has just stepped out of the room. Leaning over and giving the hat a friendly pat Ruth talks about her first successful consultation with her ghostly decorator. "I said to him, 'You know the finances and the funds. Do you think we can find a twenty-one-by-fourteen-foot rug for the dining room at a fair price?' That was my first experience and he did!"

Visions of magic carpets à la *Arabian Nights* floating through the door notwithstanding, the actual feat was accomplished minus the overt dramatics. The source for the perfect dining-room floor covering "came" to Ruth via a little subliminal message from Mr. Johnson. She immediately headed to the store and found precisely what she needed—a rug at a discounted price. Ruth laughs at the notion that it was merely a lucky coincidence. She and Mr. Johnson have been at this for quite some time.

Ruth tracks her love of Mr. Johnson's house back to the 1950s when she met then-owner Louella Wieland. Acting as a mentor for the young Ruth Bodenheimer, Ms. Wieland taught her protégée that a woman can do things on her own and in 1986 encouraged her to purchase a half-interest in the landmark building.

Three years later, in 1989, Ruth was able to secure financing to buy the remaining half of the home, becoming the sole owner—or so she thought. Louella Wieland neglected to mention the haunting presence of a third party to their arrangement. Ruth's "new" housemate sedately went about his business—until she set about making the dust fly.

Louella Wieland had been meticulous in overseeing structural repairs to the exterior of the historic Esplanade townhouse, but decorating was not her forte; the interior of the 12,000-square-foot residence was a haphazard affair. "The whole time she lived here I don't believe she put curtains on the windows or rugs on the floor," says Ruth, describing Louella Wieland's bare-bones style.

A suite of three rooms on the second floor was first on Ruth's decorating agenda, for this was to be her private living quarters. As an executive at a local steamboat company, she was known for her organizational skills and quickly applied her talent for making the impossible a reality at her new home. However, the specter of Mr. Johnson was less confident in her capabilities and clearly felt that Ruth needed a guiding hand to ensure that his impeccable taste in interior design was followed to the letter. He left a lengthy paper trail as a ghostly template for her to follow.

As Ruth began rummaging in the attic she discovered a large number of books with curiously earmarked passages. "I was finding these books Mr. Johnson left behind. . . . I learned he had a passion for drapes, carpeting, upholstered furniture. . . ." Having previously worked at a large New Orleans auction house, Ruth was especially thrilled to realize she and Mr. J. shared a love of Victorian antiques. For her, the books were Mr. Johnson's means of communication, the method he utilized to point her in the right direction. "To sit at two o'clock in the morning and read a book he underscored, it told you exactly what he was thinking." Ruth reverently picks up an 1878 edition of *Modern Dwellings in Town and Country*, showing where Mr. Johnson marked sections on how to arrange the furniture in the rooms. All of her "reference books" bear the spidery signature of *Charles Andrew Johnson* or, if he was in a hurry, the initials *C. A. J.*

The well-to-do bachelor was also fond of travel, making numerous trips to London and Paris. Gently caressing another book, Ruth points to Johnson's notations in the margins commenting on his specific preferences in food, lodging, and architecture. He was a man, she believes, who spent a great deal of time observing details and now, to Ruth's intense delight, he keeps his keen eye focused on her. "I always talk freely in front of Mr. Johnson, because I feel at some point in time, if it's a question that I have, if it's something I want to know about the house, somewhere the answer is going to appear, whether I'm reading one of his books or just wandering through the rooms. His fingerprints are all over the house."

It is not unusual, says the dignified owner of the Lanaux

Mansion, to find her at two o'clock in the morning sitting downstairs in the gold-draped parlor dominated by an ebonized nine-foot grand piano—waiting for a signal from Mr. Johnson. "I think I am carrying on the decorating of the house as close as it's ever been to 100 years ago," but, states Ruth Bodenheimer with no hesitation, "I think I would have liked his decorating better."

Ruth is committed to pleasing her ghostly decorator. In 1991, she hosted a party to commemorate his 172nd birthday. The celebration also marked the return of Mr. Johnson's portrait, which had been removed from the home in 1953, the year the Lanaux family moved away. The invitation to the birthday celebration read: *Welcome home Mr. Johnson. You have been absent thirty-eight years.*

The portrait also cleared up a mystery bothering Ruth. The one and only time this very practical woman had seen a physical manifestation of a ghost in the house, she wasn't positive who, or what, she was looking at. "It was a typical Saturday morning, and of course I was very busy working upstairs, and I came out of my bedroom and started down the hall to get something on the first floor." As Ruth reached the landing to the stairwell, something caught her attention. "It" was slowing ascending the staircase to the attic on the third floor. "I saw a vision, sort of a very misty vision. I wasn't frightened by it."

Three months later, Ruth got a call from a member of the Lanaux family, who heard she was restoring the home and told her his father, eighty-five-year-old Gaston Lanaux, had the original portrait of Charles A. Johnson. Ruth immediately went to see the portrait and came face to face with her ghostly manifestation on the stairs. "The vision I saw was of a man wearing a short jacket, like an English walking coat, cropped right above his knees. And when I saw Mr. Johnson's portrait that's what he had on." After promising to rehang the 1885 oil painting in its original position in the parlor, Ruth was able to "bring Mr. Johnson back home."

Thinking back on her ghostly vision on the stairs, Ruth Bodenheimer's face glows. "It was definitely Mr. Johnson. I think he was saying to me, 'I know how hard you work on this house and I know it's a pleasure of insanity. Good job.'" With a satisfied laugh, she adds, "I really think he was trying to tell me that."

The single sighting of her phantom housemate is a slight disappointment, but, surmises Ruth, he is probably just a little shy. "He was a very private man. He had no children." Consequently, Ruth believes, he poured all his love into, and continues to devote himself to, his home.

Yet there is still another unresolved mystery connected to Mr. Johnson's residence. To offset restoration and operating costs, Ruth Bodenheimer with her husband, Ken, opened the hundred-plus-year-old-home to bed and breakfast guests. They needed a name befitting this impressive heirloom of nineteenth-century New Orleans, and one that would lure visitors.

Poring over notarial records and Mr. Johnson's papers, Ruth discovered that the bachelor had bequeathed his home to a lovely young woman. Curious, Ruth delved a little further into her ghost's personal affairs. "In 1896 when Mr. Johnson was gravely ill, he invited Marie Andree Lanaux to move into his house to care for him." Ruth is quick to explain that all proprieties were observed. "At that particular time, Marie was married to George Lanaux and had one child. When Mr. Johnson passed away in the home, Marie inherited his entire estate, including the house. Marie had four additional children, and she lived here until her death."

If Ruth knows more about the link between the older Charles Andrew Johnson and the younger Marie Andree Lanaux, she's not telling. However, in a 1994 interview for a local paper, Ruth did allude to a mysterious envelope listed among the possessions in Mr. Johnson's will. The contents of the envelope will never be known, as the instructions written in Charles Andrew Johnson's distinct script clearly stipulated, "The envelope is to be destroyed unopened upon my death." The house on Esplanade and Chartres is the only tangible proof of Johnson's devotion to Marie.

Ruth Bodenheimer christened the home the Lanaux Mansion because there were so many generations of Lanauxs who had grown up in the home and, she concedes, it has a more evocative ring than the more mundane-sounding "Johnson House."

In spite of this bit of fudging with names, Ruth remains steadfastly loyal to Mr. Johnson. Guests given a guided tour of the formal rooms on the first floor are always first presented to a gold-framed likeness of the distinguished gentleman seated in the parlor, coat precisely arranged and spectacles in hand. Ruth admits she speaks so often in the present tense of Mr. Johnson, many people believe he is a flesh and blood family member living in the home. She pokes fun at those who look at his portrait and claim they too can sense his presence, because they feel a warm spot in the room. Says a smiling Ruth, "The room is warm because I have the heat on."

Ruth holds out hope that Mr. Johnson will overcome his shyness and put in another personal appearance. "I would like to think that Mr. Johnson could walk through that door this evening and I would be so glad to see him. I wouldn't think that strange at all." In the meantime, she remains grateful to her ghostly housemate for his impeccable decorating tips.

Ruth Bodenheimer identifies so closely with Mr. Johnson's era that she inadvertently began her interview for the television documentary with "When *I* first moved here in *1896*..." Ruth just shrugs at the Freudian slip teleporting her back a hundred years. "Some people might think I'm absolutely crazy," acknowledges the serene owner of the Lanaux Mansion, who firmly believes that "the past is part of us today."

Three ghosts claimed this former French Quarter pub as their private haunting grounds.

14

Celtic Love Triangle

Carried by waves of Irish immigrants from the 1840s through the 1860s, Celtic legends arrived in New Orleans, adding to the port city's mystique. While some might find it odd to discover an authentic Irish pub in the heart of the French Quarter, the haunting ballads that are the hallmarks of Irish culture offer the perfect balm for three spirits who claim this entertaining spot as their own. Angelique, Joseph and Mary form a ghostly triumvirate that has refused to be "cleared" from the property.

Entrance to O'Flaherty's Irish Channel Pub on the first block of Toulouse Street is through a brick-lined arched carriage way joining two historic buildings. Ducking under a sea of flags representing the seven Celtic nations—Ireland, Scotland, Wales, Cornwall, the Isle of Man, Brittany, and Galicia—visitors are intrigued to find themselves in a charming Spanish-style courtyard complete with a triple-tiered fountain. When Irish balladeer Danny O'Flaherty went shopping in 1985 for a site for his new music club, the combination of the courtyard fountain and historic buildings proved irresistible. "It looked like Galway City; it reminded me of home—the doors, the windows, the arches are just like some of the Spanish architecture in Galway," affirms the transplanted Irishman. Danny grew up with his sisters and brothers in the rugged Gaeltecht region of western Ireland, where myths of fairies and leprechauns still exert a powerful hold over the land and its people.

Preoccupied with transforming the circa-1800 New Orleans complex into a pub and restaurant, Danny was unaware at first that his long-term lease included a built-in audience of troubled spirits. Given a choice of which ghost he'd rather play for, Danny favors Angelique. "Angelique, God bless her, she watches us play music. Now I haven't seen her myself because I can't be looking upstairs and singing all the time, but my staff tells me that everytime I sing certain songs, she appears. In that way, we've gotten to know each other very well."

When not on tour, Danny O'Flaherty and The Celtic Folk play weekend nights in the Ballad Room, a special performance venue to the right of the main entrance. The ceiling of the Ballad Room has been cut out, exposing the timbered beams of the second-floor entresol level. From this high vantage point, the diaphanous apparition of Angelique peers down over the heads of the performers and the audience. As Danny reaches into his back left pocket to pull out a tin whistle, Angelique settles in. The lilting notes from Danny's Irish flute weave their own magic spell, holding the fragile figure captive. Her sighs are palpable, for Danny's soulful rendition of a traditional Scottish ballad rekindles the pain of her lover's betrayal. "If my true love she were gone, I would surely find another. Where wild mountain thyme grows, around the blooming heather, will ye go, lassie, go?" The lyrics usually prove too much for the tenderhearted Angelique. Smiling sadly at the Irish balladeer below, she takes her leave.

Repeated complaints—from his bartenders, waitresses, family, and friends—of ghostly interruptions, both gentle and rude, forced the singer/songwriter to dig into the matter. Danny headed straight for the Historic New Orleans Collection, a vast repository of information about the city and its inhabitants.

From 1722 to 1795, the property passed through a series of owners. Intrigued by his research, Danny discovers an advertisement dated August 21, 1802: *For Sale. A house situated in the street of the Government House [Toulouse Street] built of brick and roofed with tiles . . . there are in the said house a store . . . two fine apartments . . . a brick kitchen on which is an upper story. Apply to M. Bastien Estevan, proprietor, who lives there.* Reading between the notarial lines, it is clear to the Irish bard that the next recorded act of sale set in motion the haunted love triangle.

On March 3, 1803, Don Guillaume Marre affixes his name to the deed. Don Guillaume has recently wed a stunning widow, Mary Wheaton Sevre of Cumberland, New Jersey. Three years later, a notation dated October 13, 1806, reveals that the aforementioned widow, Mary Wheaton Sevre, is now sole owner of the property by virtue of the death of her second husband, Don Guillaume Marre. The widow Marre wasted no time in picking out husband number three, Joseph Baptandiere, native of Aute Luce, Mont Blanc, France. In marrying Joseph, the merry widow Mary apparently met her match.

Reared in the small fishing village of Connemara outside of Galway, Danny O'Flaherty learned from an early age to trust his instincts, and his instincts told him the hauntings somehow centered on the marrying Mary. "I think probably that every tribe that God has created is very superstitious, but Irish beliefs are very unique." In a heavy brogue that colors his speech with the wild beauty of the Emerald Isle, Danny speaks of an ancient landscape populated by Celts, Druids, and little people. "You know, I can take any nonbeliever back to Ireland during the winter and I tell you, it wouldn't take more than forty-eight hours for he or she to be afraid of the landscape at nightime . . . there's something about the air, the surroundings in Ireland that's different than any other place in the world. I don't know whether we're more or less superstitious than anybody else, but I think probably that there are *things* living there, and we see them."

What Danny saw when he read of the marriage between Mary and Joseph, husband number three, was trouble. And the trouble arrived in the dark Creole beauty of Angelique.

In late eighteenth- and early nineteenth-century New Orleans, there was a common practice known as *plaçage*; this arrangement involved wealthy White, often married, gentlemen and free women of color, *demoiselles de couleur.* Author Mary Gehman explains in *The Free People of Color of New Orleans* that these liaisons often lasted a lifetime and the women involved viewed themselves as their White protectors' "other" wives. A woman living in such an arrangement was a *placée*, from the French "placed"; her benefactor usually set her up with a house.

As Danny O'Flaherty was to discover, Angelique Dubois and Joseph Baptandiere had entered into a mutually beneficial mode of *plaçage*. But, there was a hitch. Angelique was madly in love with Joseph and desired to be his real wife. Joseph had managed to keep his liaison with Angelique from Mary, who he knew from experience was not one to look the other way. The inevitable happened.

There is nothing like a bewitching curly-haired, blue-eyed bard to lift a love triangle gone awry to the level of epic prose, but such is the consummate skill of one Daniel J. O'Flaherty. "One day they were having a rout [Danny transforms this one-syllable euphemism for "fight" into an entire nine-round boxing match] and Angelique said she was going to tell on him to Mary, his wife. And he didn't know how to take it. And I believe he strangled her to death; he killed her. And he buried Angelique in the courtyard." Danny indicates a small raised spot in the garden lining the rear wall. Nearby, couples sip their drinks in the peaceful courtyard under a canopy of trees strung with miniature lights, unaware of Angelique's final abode.

However, on the night of the murder, there was a witness. "This little teenage boy saw him digging the grave, and Joseph saw the boy. So he knew the cat was out of the bag and he couldn't face Mary. He went up to the third floor, put a rope around his neck, and jumped off the building. And ever since then, his spirit has never left." Empathizing with the woeful ghost of Joseph, Danny declares, "He can be very grouchy. If I jumped off the third floor, I'd be grouchy myself, whether I was living or dead."

Today the third floor of the Creole townhouse is used for storage of odds and ends. The wide-plank floors are covered in dust and pitted with holes; the brick fireplaces are barren, stripped of their cypress mantels. O'Flaherty's employees reluctantly venture up to the third level only to untangle a

Celtic flag trapped in the balcony railings outside the former master bedroom.

Danny's siblings are also adamant about avoiding the upper floors of their brother's pub. "My sisters won't go up on the third floor at all anymore," says Danny. "Ann Marie once went up there and saw Angelique, and Kathleen heard strange noises on the third floor. You know it's no wonder Ann Marie went back to Ireland and Kathleen is in Chicago. They left me and my brother Patrick by ourselves."

There is some debate about which ghost is going out of his/her way to frighten people off. The murder/suicide of Angelique and Joseph happened in 1810. The disposition of Mary Wheaton Sevre Marre Baptandiere's will took place in probate court on March 15, 1817.

A few of the regular patrons at O'Flaherty's talk about a spirit who rattles around the buildings throwing temper tantrums. They believe it's the jealous Mary, still in a rage over her husband's affair with Angelique. In one extreme instance, books flew off of the shelves in the Celtic Gift Shop, located in the service building at the rear of the courtyard. The angry ghost seemed to be aiming at an attractive female customer who had the misfortune of entering the shop at an inopportune moment. As the story makes the rounds at the bar, the regulars down their glasses of Guinness in the familiar "I-told-you-so camaraderie" of ones who have seen it all before.

Wrapped in the embrace of "Ol' Man River," the Crescent City nurtures a love of exotic cultures and characters that is insatiable. When word got out that the Irish pub on Toulouse Street was haunted, ghost tours flocked to O'Flaherty's. A Japanese film crew camped out overnight, attempting to be the first to capture the ghosts in action. The syndicated television show "Strange Universe" aired feature stories (shot by photographer Oak Lea) on the paranormal phenomena at the pub, and budding parapsychologists poured through, hoping to experience a psychic encounter.

But the ghost business and the music business began to hit

a few sour notes. "I thought the ghosts were going to go on strike because of the way people were fighting over them," stated Danny in the midst of the fray. The competition for rights to call on O'Flaherty's ghosts was also wreaking havoc on the pub's paying customers. As more and more haunted-tour guides arrived with their groups in tow and blockaded the courtyard, Celtic music fans were jostled aside. Danny's older brother Patrick, himself a fine musician, indeed known as "the finest mandolin player on the planet," had enough.

Things came to a head when haunted-tour guides complained that the music from the Ballad Room and the Informer Pub was disturbing their psychic connections with the ghosts. The ghost guides demanded absolute silence when they laid their hands on the "cold" spot in the courtyard over Angelique's grave. Negotiations for a peaceful resolution between musicians and ghost hunters failed; the ghost tours were banned from O'Flaherty's.

Former *Times-Picayune* newspaper columnist Christopher Rose compared the battle over which haunted-tour business had the inside track to a specific ghost to "a real-life game of Dungeons and Dragons." Rose's article, "The Invasion of the Tourist Snatchers," captured the frenzy erupting in the lucrative ghost industry. "There is no shortage of go-cup-clutching middle Americans eager to plop down $15 to hear tales of the city's dark and lusty past."

To ensure that no other tour group could profit from the haunted spirits at O'Flaherty's, one enterprising parapsychologist performed what he called a "clearing" on the property. He announced in his company's newsletter that "from a scientific point of view it is unfortunate to no longer have such a laboratory [to provide] valuable data to aid in the field of Paranormal research." O'Flaherty's ghosts were declared to have vacated the premises—*personae non gratae*. In short, if the parapsychologist's company couldn't have access to the spirits of the dead at the pub, then with a little skilled sorcery, no one else could either.

Meanwhile, Danny O'Flaherty had a surprise announcement

of his own. It seems that after the psychic clearing, Angelique, Joseph, and Mary took a little trip. A couple of hundred years of haunting the same venue proved a little tiresome. Seeking a change of pace, they flitted about, checking out other music clubs around the globe. But lo and behold, declares the mischievous Irishman, they missed the cozy ambiance of his Irish pub and . . . "they're baaack!"

For Danny O'Flaherty the whole issue of ghosts is really quite simple. "There are two ways of looking at it—you can live with them, or you can be afraid the rest of your life." And with wry humor O'Flaherty slips in, "If you can get a happy medium, you're in great shape."

Like a skilled stepdancer, Danny O'Flaherty does a lively jig hopping over controversial issues and smoothing the waters. He would prefer not to offend anyone, but there are certain traditions, ceremonies, and symbols this true son of the old country will never be without. Besides the requisite St. Patrick's Day shenanigans and decorations, a currach (in local parlance, an Irish pirogue or rowing skiff) is strapped permanently to the ceiling over the bar, and the walls are emblazoned with shields bearing the coats of arms of the counties in Ireland. The establishment is opened each day with a ritual page turning of the *Book of Kells,* which is locked in a special alcove under the stairs. Steaming plates of shepherd's pie and Irish stew are mainstays on the menu, and Celtic folk tunes—jigs, sea chanteys, ballads, hornpipes, and reels—are the only music allowed. As proof that the old ways live, Danny also insists on observing Celtic New Year, Samhain, on Halloween.

The ancient Celtic calendar marked the eve of October 31 through the dawning of November 1 as the high Feast of Samhain (rhymes with *cow*-in). This was the most important time in the Celtic year as winter and summer were the two defining seasons. Thus Samhain ("Sam"—end of; "hain"—summer) marked the end of the old year and the beginning of the new. It was also a time of great personal danger, for in the waning hours of October 31, it was believed that the barriers between the natural and supernatural worlds were lowered and the creatures of the other world were free to roam, visible to mankind.

"During Samhain, it's the closest you can be to the dead. On October 31 the dead can come back and visit—sit in your living room, if they want." And just as you would do for any company, "food would be laid out for them, for the dead, and we do it every Celtic New Year's Eve here at O'Flaherty's as well," explains the generous Mr. O'Flaherty. "We put tables full of food in the courtyard and we talk to the dead, or you can talk to someone in the family that came before you. And we wish them well. It's an old Celtic custom." It is little wonder that Angelique, Joseph, and Mary came back—a roof over their heads, music *and* food in abundance. That's pretty good service for a trio of ghosts.

O'Flaherty, the Irish impresario, does offer a few words of caution to those who set out to lure ghosts to their table. Spirits of the dead and other mystical creatures possess extraordinary powers on October 31 and are particularly fond of tricking humans. In Ireland, "fairies can be pretty mean," says Danny. "They would abduct you, kidnap you, and take you to their mounds, where you would be trapped forever." So the O'Flaherty children learned, like others in their village, to try and disguise themselves that night. "If you were wearing a coat, for instance, you turn the coat inside out so they wouldn't recognize you. Or if you're standing on some kind of dirt, you get that dirt underneath your shoes and you throw it at them and they would leave you alone. Us little wee ones, we were afraid, and I'll put it to you this way, there wasn't many people in my village that would go out that night because you might meet your relative that was gone before you. So people would light a candle for their deceased loved ones in their house—or those that were brave would put the candle on the grave where the person had died."

Listening to Danny lay out the past is like embarking on a breathless voyage through time. The centuries peel away. You're standing on the jagged cliffs of the Aran Islands; the sea is battering the shoreline. Bonfires are lit to encourage the warmth of the sun and hold back the darkness of the coming winter months. All about you, children in coarse shapeless robes the color of the earth are scrambling for more peat for the bonfires.

To confuse and frighten off the dead emerging from their dank graves, the adults don animal skins, wave sticks above their heads, and growl ferociously. Others are carving out turnips to hold a flicker of light from the bonfire. As they fashion these portable torches, the light catches and eerie faces grin from the hollowed-out roots. It is only with the arrival of the pink-seared dawn that the Druid families relax their guard. The old year has been laid to rest, the dead have returned to their graves, and the ancient Celts greet the new year with a collective sigh of relief—the Feast of Samhain is over.

Back in the present, you realize with startling clarity that Halloween is not just some make-believe children's game played out in Kmart plastic costumes and candy trick-or-treat scavenger hunts. The Celtic Feast of Samhain never died; it was just conveniently appropriated. Early Christian leaders found it was far easier to change the meaning of a celebration than to eliminate it. The 31st of October was dubbed All Souls' Day and declared a hallowed evening. The dawn of the first day of the Celtic New Year, November 1, was transformed into All Saints' Day.

Fr. William Maestri, a former Catholic moral theologian, sums up the Christian sleight-of-hand conversion of Halloween. "What you have here on All Saints' Day and All Souls' Day, especially All Souls' Day, is the great Catholic genius of 'if there's something good about it, we'll grab it, baptize it, claim it as our own, and claim we invented it.'" With his gray hair cropped to within a half-inch of his scalp, a complexion so fair it defies description, and a skeletal frame wrapped in an innocuous black shirt and trousers, Father Maestri demands your undivided attention, for you fear if you look away for even the briefest instant, he will simply dissolve into particles of dust. Then his blue-gray eyes home in and this dynamic personality cuts through layers of dogma. "Catholics talk about all saints, whom we remember as all the good dead who have died, and we celebrate them and keep their memory alive because we believe they're with God anyway. And secondly, all souls, we pray for all of those who have died, that they may ultimately reside in the mercy of God. *Not* that they're going to be sent back to us. *Not* that they're going to make contact. . . . Ultimately what we want for them is we want them to rest in peace. . . . What you have in the idea of Halloween and these kinds of things is a human attempt to take the terror out of death. And how do you do it? Well, you make a costume. You make it a ritual. Ritual is one way we control the uncontrollable."

Christian-centuries later, Power Rangers, Superman, and Xena, Princess Warrior costumes replace animal skins, plastic jack-o'-lanterns and pumpkins have taken over for the turnip torches, and hordes of children out trick or treating are a less threatening version of the hijinks instigated by kidnapping fairies. The modern celebration of Halloween remains the only true Celtic holiday observed without interruption through the ebb and flow of time.

Sadly, O'Flaherty's Irish Channel Pub did not reopen after Hurricane Katrina. Happily, New Orleans Creole Cookery, a fine dining establishment, refurbished the buildings and courtyard. According to the new owners, the spirits of Angelique, Joseph, and Mary were not disturbed and remain comfortably ensconced.

15

The Madam Who Won't Lie Still

They called it Storyville, but fairytales in "The District" were few and far between. In its heyday from 1897 to 1917, vice flourished and prostitution had a place to call home. The reigning madam of New Orleans' red-light district was the flamboyant Josie Arlington. Historian Henri Gandolfo dubbed her "The Prima Donna of Storyville," for she insisted on calling all the shots—right to the end, micromanaging her own funeral. The ghost of Josie Arlington may still be out and about. It seems Madam Josie has some unfinished business near her grave at Metairie Cemetery.

Born Mamie Duebler somewhere around 1864 (a woman never divulges her real age), Josie, called "little Mary," grew up in the Carrollton section of New Orleans. Her conservative, God-fearing parents were certainly distraught when seventeen-year-old Mamie ran away to become the mistress of Philip ("The Schwarz") Lobrano. For the next nine years, gentlemen callers could find this former uptown girl, working under the name Josie Alton, within the darkened rooms of some of New Orleans' most notorious brothels.

Josie was a fiery beauty with a temper to match. Her numerous brawls quickly escalated from name calling to all-out physical assaults. Herbert Asbury, in his 1936 exposé of the tawdry side of the old French Quarter reports, that in one particularly violent 1886 street fight with a "prostitute, Beulah Ripley," Josie lost most of her hair while Beulah "staggered from the scene of combat minus part of her lower lip and half of her ear." Whom or what they were fighting over, time has swept away.

Madam Josie Arlington designed her own elaborate tomb. (Courtesy of Danielle Genter)

Josie was also fond of reinventing herself. In 1886, tired of having to fork over a share of her earnings, she set up her own shop at 172 Customhouse Street (now Iberville in the Vieux Carré). She called herself Josie Lobrano, but in many ways nothing changed. Her "girls," following their "madam's" lead, were just as contentious; her brothel was the scene of many a bloody "cat fight." Digging into the newspapers and court records of the day, Asbury discovered that Josie's peculiar living arrangements included supporting not only her "fancy man" Schwarz Lobrano, but several members of her family. During the course of one memorable altercation, everyone got in on the act. It ended when Lobrano shot Josie's brother, Peter Duebler. Lobrano was arrested. The first hearing was a fiasco and ended in a mistrial. At his second trial, Philip ("The Schwarz") Lobrano was acquitted, but by then, even the brawling Josie had enough. She kicked everyone out and closed up shop.

The irrepressible Josie next tried a little bait-and-switch tactic to lure a more refined customer. In 1895, an announcement ran in *The Mascot* alerting interested parties to the arrival of a "bona-fide baroness, direct from the Court at St. Petersburg." Said baroness would receive visitors at the "Chateau Lobrano d'Arlington" at the same Customhouse Street address as Josie's old bordello. Josie, reincarnated for the third time as Josie Lobrano d'Arlington, would "facilitate" introductions to the baroness, who preferred to remain incognito and should be addressed as "La Belle Stewart." Gentlemen flocked to Josie's revamped establishment for the opportunity of "meeting" the baroness and a group of other similarly "titled royal ladies." It was an interesting ploy, until the baroness was unveiled as a former sideshow circus performer.

Josie's next go-round was her finest hour in the business. With the money she raked in during the era of the baroness, she went on to build the "grandest and gaudiest" bordello in Storyville.

Prostitution had made inroads into Louisiana almost from the colony's inception. The reigning French monarchs Louis XIV and Louis XV shipped hordes of convicts and prostitutes to their newly acquired territory in hopes of colonizing the vast wasteland. Shortly after the Louisiana Purchase, gamblers, traders, and rough and rowdy keelboatmen descended on the bustling port city of New Orleans. Knowing that the pockets of these arrivals were lined with ready cash, members of the world's oldest profession moved in to service them. New Orleans was fast becoming the wild west of prostitution.

In 1897 a well-meaning alderman (city council member), one Sidney Story, made an exhaustive study to determine how large European cities handled similar dilemmas. Story introduced an ordinance to contain prostitution and prevent houses of ill repute from encroaching into respectable neighborhoods. The Story ordinance decreed: "Be it ordained by the Common Council of the City of New Orleans . . . Section I of Ordinance 13,032 C.S. . . . From and after the first of October, 1897, it shall be unlawful for any prostitute or woman notoriously abandoned to lewdness, to occupy, inhabit, live or sleep in any house, room or closet, situated without the following limits, viz: From the South side of Customhouse Street to the North side of St. Louis Street, and from the lower or wood side of North Basin Street to the lower or wood side of Robertson Street [in the French Quarter]."

The ordinance did not legalize gambling, but sought to contain the "red-light district" to a single area of town, and in the time-honored tradition, only the women were restricted in their movements; no such restraints were put on the men who sought them out. The ordinance was amended in January of 1898 to further make it unlawful outside of this same thirty-eight-block area to "open, operate or carry on any cabaret, concert-saloon or place where *can can* . . . or similar female dancing are shown." The councilman's ordinance created a city within a city where prostitutes could ply their trade safe from the interference of the police. Much to the disgust of the morally upright Sidney Story, the nation's most celebrated red-light district became widely known as "Storyville," a dubious honor he would take to his grave. Storyville came complete with its own Yellow Pages. Dubbed "The Blue Book," it allowed the prospective gentleman caller to "let his fingers do the walking" through a racy assortment of advertisements, illustrations, and hype about "star performers."

The entrepreneurial madam Josie caught on quickly and had already made nice with the political boss of the Fourth Ward (which included Storyville), Thomas C. Anderson. Anderson was a two-term member of the Louisiana legislature, unofficial mayor of the unofficial town of Storyville, and owner of several prosperous bordellos and saloons. Shedding all her previous aliases (Duebler, Alton, Lobrano), Josie now simply called herself Josie Arlington, in honor of Anderson's favorite saloon, the Arlington Annex at the corner of Customhouse and North Basin streets.

Setting up shop in new digs at 215 Basin Street, Josie also christened her fashionable four-story house "The Arlington." Bay windows on three sides, a domed cupola on the roof, intricate gingerbread painted a pristine white—the exterior created the illusion of a chaste Victorian maiden. Inside all such restraints were off. The interior decor erupted into a riot of gilt, purple-velvet drapes, oriental carpets, green-damask chairs and sofas, silver doorknobs, lace curtains, beveled mirrors, cut-glass chandeliers, and bric-a-brac stuffed into every shelf and corner.

Josie's new girls were a far cry from the squabbling unkempt women at her old brothel on Customhouse Street or the fake baroness/sideshow freak of her last scam. At The Arlington, Josie had no fewer than ten "exquisite strumpets," and during Mardi Gras season, the number doubled. The Arlington was the "crème de la crème" of bordellos and Josie Arlington was regarded as "the snootiest madam in America."

With her steady cash flow, the "Snooty Madam" purchased a $35,000 home on Esplanade Avenue, smack in the middle of respectable society. Her shocked female neighbors pointedly ignored her presence. Clearly unimpressed with their disdain, Madam Josie swept by them, smug in the knowledge that she would soon be entertaining their eager husbands in her business establishment on Basin Street.

For the next eight years, Josie Arlington reveled in her role as the "First Lady of Storyville." But in 1905, a fire of unknown origins rocked her world. It caused such severe damage to the interior of The Arlington that Josie was forced to move her girls and set up temporary shop on the second floor of her friend Tom Anderson's saloon. However, the most devastating effect on Josie was psychological. Having narrowly escaped death, she became obsessed with making preparations for her final passing. Unlike most folks, Josie was not concerned for her immortal soul, but rather the disposition of her physical remains. She believed that her final resting place, like her highly touted business establishment and her private mansion on fashionable Esplanade Avenue, must be a lasting monument to her sense of style and a signal to all that little Mamie Duebler had made it on her own.

For more than sixty-five years the late Henri Gandolfo, historian and scholar par excellence, wrote and lectured on New Orleans' unique Cities of the Dead. The elaborate tombs and cenotaphs spoke volumes to this gifted storyteller. Gandolfo knew every intimate secret, every scandal, every tantalizing bit of gossip about the bodies buried therein. And Gandolfo had the inside scoop on Josie Arlington.

Josie, says Gandolfo, purchased a $2,000 plot in Metairie Cemetery surrounded by the tombs of the social elite of the city. She next summoned Albert Weiblen, the leading builder and designer of tombs, to her Esplanade home. He arrived bearing a portfolio of black and white sketches based on classical tomb designs in Munich, Germany. After a lengthy meeting, Weiblen contracted an Italian artist named Orsini to make a full color drawing of Josie's proposed mausoleum. With the Storyville madam's stamp of approval, Weiblen hired a small army of workers to erect the tomb in record time. As a reward for meeting her deadline, Josie hosted an extravagant champagne supper for the exhausted workmen.

Josie's design choice—almost a self-portrait—was an oddly prophetic one, stirring an epoch of controversy. Carved from highly polished reddish-brown marble from Stonington,

Maine, the striking tomb sits on a small grassy mound roped off with a looped chain of cast iron. Two simple pilasters frame the immense double bronze doors of the crypt. These pillars are capped with matching square urns, each holding what some would like to believe are carved renditions of the eternal flame of life. The flip side of this lofty interpretation falls back on the early days of prostitution in New Orleans. Flambeaux, or torches, were lit outside small hovels or cribs on Gallatin Street adjacent to the river to let potential customers know the prostitute was in and open for business. Red lights are a universal symbol for danger and the term "red-light district" is part of the worldwide lexicon—a designated area for vice and prostitution. Josie's urns, with their plumes leaning heavily to the right, give the illusion they have just received a mighty blow from a hefty gust of wind off the river.

If Josie selected these symbolic torches to represent her chosen profession, or they were simply part of Weiblen's concept, we will never know. But these are minor touches compared to the life-size bronze statue of a woman standing just outside the tomb.

The controversial statue was created by German sculptor F. Bagdon in 1911. Artfully draped in a flowing Grecian gown, the voluptuous full figure commands attention. The statue's right foot is poised just inches from the door, while the left leg is one step down. In her left arm, the female statue holds a bouquet of roses, but it is her right arm that generates the most gossip. Reaching forward, her fingertips almost, but not quite, touch the door. "See," say sympathetic insiders, "it's poor Josie locked out again by her heartless father. She's stuck outside, banging on the door trying to get back in!" Those who live near Metairie Cemetery swear the statue of the maiden comes back to life "angrily pounding the slab with both metallic fists with a din that may be heard for blocks."

Support for the rationale behind the compelling statue is captured in *Gumbo Ya-Ya*, a delightful collection of some of Louisiana's most popular folktales. Editors Lyle Saxon, Edward Dreyer, and Robert Tallant believe that Josie's troubles can all be heaped on dear old Dad: seventeen-year-old Josie (Mamie Duebler) did not run away at all. Like most teenage girls, she stayed out beyond curfew one evening and her father locked her out. Ignoring his daughter's anguished pleas, the stubborn Mr. Duebler refused to let her back in. Vowing that no one would ever slam a door in her face again, young Mamie embarked on a career that would ensure her financial independence. Josie (the former Mamie) would now and forever be in control of her own destiny.

This same terror of being locked out in life carried over to Josie's careful preparations for her final resting place. It would be the ultimate irony if Josie Arlington was condemned to pounding for admittance to her own grave.

This interpretation is rejected by the self-righteous who prefer to think that the statue is actually an apt representation of "Josie, The Scarlet Harlot, knocking in vain at the gates of heaven."

All sides overlook the facts: Josie Arlington personally selected every detail of her own memorial, making sure there would always be a place for her; Madam Arlington would have no desire to see herself depicted ad infinitum as a helpless young girl denied admittance by a cruel papa, or banned at the pearly gates by a stern archangel.

A closer look at the bronze figure reveals no signs of distress: her face is serene; her fingers are relaxed; she is neither pulling on the large ringed doorknockers nor pounding with her fists. This is a self-assured, sensuous woman returning from a stroll in the garden, eager to fill the interior of her lasting abode with the aroma of freshly picked flowers.

A much-quoted tale, first published in 1945 in *Gumbo Ya-Ya: Folk Tales of Louisiana*, unequivocally states, "Twice the Maiden has taken walks." At night the statue turns, travels down the five granite steps, and meanders about the grounds. The ghost of Josie making house calls? Josie looking up old friends?

In *Metairie Cemetery—An Historical Memoir*, author Henri Gandolfo reveals one final tidbit about Miss Josie Arlington. It seems that the Storyville madam who spent her life in the company of men never intended to sleep alone for all eternity;

Josie specifically instructed builder Weiblen to expand the original design to accommodate two burial vaults. The unnamed intended co-occupant never had a chance to move in.

In spite of Josie's well-laid plans, her funeral and its aftermath were a fiasco. Josie died on February 14, 1914, three years after the completion of her tomb. She was at best estimates fifty years old. While the grave was awash with flowers from anonymous "benefactors," the service was sparsely attended: Tom Anderson, the "mayor" of Storyville, John T. Brady, her personal manager, a civil court judge, and a priest.

That evening, with Josie's body barely settled in, a passerby was awestruck by the phenomenon blazing before him. The two granite flambeaux atop the columns on the Storyville madam's tomb were flickering a brilliant red. Crowds gathered to witness the spectacle. "Look—Josie's open for business!" they shouted. Night after night curious hordes of people, convinced that Josie had set up shop and was accepting callers in the afterlife, converged on the shell road running alongside the cemetery. Historian Gandolfo comments sardonically that "entertainment must have been hard to come by in those days." To maintain order, police detachments had to remain on duty all night.

Metairie Cemetery officials were mortified by this unseemly state of affairs and scrambled to find a way to halt it. Finally one astute cemetery worker noticed a recently installed light at the toll barrier of the nearby New Basin Shell Road. As the beacon swung in the breeze, its beam bounced off the polished granite of Josie's tomb. Gandolfo notes that while the reflection of the beacon did spill over to other nearby tombs, "it was only the Duebler [Arlington] tomb that provided the supernatural display" of flashing light. An order was quickly given to plant a massive line of shrubs as a barrier between the outside row of tombs in the cemetery and the toll beacon. A large cross was also etched on the rear of the tomb—a little Christian gris-gris to deflect the devil's work. Neither the shrubs nor the cross had any impact. Josie's tomb continued to send out its scandalous signal.

Finally, after a little negotiation with the proprietors of the toll road, the signal light was extinguished completely, effectively pulling the plug on the nocturnal display. The crowds dispersed and Josie should have been able to rest easier.

A new wrinkle arrived in the form of Josie's convent-raised niece. Following in the footsteps of her "Aunt Mamie," the young niece became enamored with her own "fancy man," John Brady, Josie's close friend and former business manager. In her will, Josie bequeathed her considerable assets to her niece and John, knowing nothing of their clandestine affair. The pair squandered their inheritance in an astonishingly short period of time, even by fun-loving New Orleans' standards. The financially strapped couple sold off Josie's magnificent private mansion on Esplanade Avenue, and when that wasn't enough, the tomb was next on the auction block!

In the only-in-New Orleans category, a prominent family purchased the tomb of the Storyville madam, naively believing that the prostitute's notoriety would magically disappear once they had their name carved in large block letters over the doors of the crypt. "Foolish mortals," the spirit of Josie chuckled. "There is nothing so enduring as a good scandal."

Naturally, before any dearly departed relative of the new owners was interred in Josie's tomb, Josie had to go. It must have been quite a sight to see workmen in the dead of night pull open the heavy bronze doors, lift the displaced madam, and whisk her body to an undisclosed location.

As gruesome as this might sound, moving bodies about is standard operating procedure in New Orleans—a burial custom practiced in the city up to and including the present day. The late Bernard ("Irv") Zoller of Lake Lawn Metairie Cemeteries explains: "It's called the year-and-a-day rule. Anytime after one year has passed, a burial can be disturbed. The casket is taken out of the vault; the remains are taken out of the casket and put into another container, which is today a small plastic pouch, like a small body bag. The casket is destroyed."

Zoller casually goes on to list several options available for the disposition of the bagged remains. "Cemetery workers, at the request of the family, will put the pouch . . . on a shelf in the back of the vault, in the lower recesses of the vault" (a small basement, if you will). "If there is space," says Zoller, the remains of the displaced family member are returned and placed "on top of the new casket." Zoller adds one final option to this list of disposal selections. "They've even put them inside the casket, if it's a spouse that's being buried." Family togetherness carried to the extreme—the new corpse gets to cradle the bagged remains of his/her previously deceased loved one.

In Josie's case none of the above was a viable alternative. The new tomb owners had no inclination to share. And given Miss Arlington's propensity to attract attention (both in life and death), cemetery officials were not about to risk a repeat performance. Josie's new burial site is, according to Henri Gandolfo, "one of Metairie Cemetery's most closely guarded secrets."

Just to the left of the original gates of the old cemetery is a white stucco, red-tiled-roof building resembling a Spanish-style church complete with bell tower. No worship services are conducted within—this is the "Receiving Vault"; it holds the bodies of those with nowhere else to go.

Many of Metairie's grandiose tombs were not finished in time. Bodies were placed in a holding pattern inside the "Receiving Vault" until the intended tomb was complete, or, in the case of someone like Josie, a body was stored here until other arrangements were made. A present-day cemetery worker, who prefers his anonymity, asserts that "numerous unclaimed bodies are stacked inside."

If Josie's body was secretly stashed here, rest assured Madam's spirit would never take such matters lying down, and her story may still have a happy ending. A charming encounter involving the spirit of Josie and a famous hero was shared with producer Barbara Sillery during the making of *The Haunting of Louisiana*.

Each year at Halloween the Friends of the Cabildo, in support of the Louisiana State Museum, host a weekend "Ghostly

Galavant" through the French Quarter. Costumed docents take on the roles of legendary New Orleans characters. On one such weekend, a slightly tipsy older woman gave her character, Josie Arlington, free rein. Regaling the tour crowded into a private courtyard with tales of her bawdy escapades at various brothels, the actress "Josie" boasted they all came to her: governors, mayors, statesmen, generals—society's finest. The docent wrapped up her performance by telling the amazing story of her burial vault. After receiving some polite clapping, the exhausted "Josie" sank onto a concrete bench. Producer Barbara Sillery leaned over to congratulate the docent on her entertaining portrayal. Looking up through watery-blue eyes, "Josie" whispered: "You know, they think it's so sad I was kicked out of my tomb and stuck somewhere else. We're having the best time."

Intrigued, Sillery asked, "We?"

"Yes," replied the rejuvenated "Josie." "Toussy and I have a lot to talk about now."

"And by Toussy you mean?" prompted Sillery.

"Why, Gen. Pierre Gustave Toutant Beauregard, of course!"

In life, the irreverent Josie was eminently the type to flirt with a handsome Confederate hero. Josie was in her prime when Beauregard returned to New Orleans after the war. When the general died at the age of seventy-five, his solemn funeral and burial in Metairie Cemetery left a lasting impression on the Storyville madam. His body was interred in the tumulus (a burial chamber built into an earthen mound) of the Benevolent Association, Army of Tennessee, Louisiana Division. By a formal act of the association, Beauregard's remains can never be removed. The slab over his crypt carries an eternal guarantee—sort of a perpetual Do Not Disturb sign.

Although she chose to be buried close by in Metairie Cemetery, the unlucky Josie, unlike the general, has a hard time staying put. Her body may have been tossed into the "Receiving Vault," but her spirit refuses to be contained. The lingering ghost of the Storyville madam seems well suited to inhabit the beautiful female form at her former tomb. And if the statue occasionally steps down for a short walk to reminisce with an old friend, could this not simply be Josie, once again taking charge? A desire to beat the odds is a powerful force.

So for Josie Arlington, wherever she may lie, a lasting epitaph:

She played all the angles; her life and death
remain glittering beacons in New Orleans' storied past.

Here in sultry Louisiana, spectral figures lure us in. (Courtesy of Danielle Genter)

Epilogue

"Things that go bump in the night" are rooted deep in Louisiana's ethnically diverse folk-life and storytelling traditions. Like the meandering Ol' Man River that defines it, Louisiana and her people follow their own ethereal rhythms, patterns, and beliefs. Their affinity and affection for homegrown ghosts continue to generate a lively debate.

Anne Fitzgerald, former owner of Loyd Hall: "It's just a part of life and part of what goes on here. We're Southerners and people tend to think that in the Deep South we're kind of crazy at times anyway. Maybe it's just the heat and humidity and overactive imaginations, but when you live in a structure such as this you have to accept the ghosts and spirits that are here, just as you accept the fact that you don't have central heat and air. Ghosts are all part of what goes to make this house a home."

Mary Louise Prudhomme, former director of the Old State Capitol Museum: "Do I think ghosts and hauntings are possible? Don't you? I think anything's possible. Yes, I believe; there's too many things that have happened here to make me know that someone else made that possible that was not associated in the physical form. I believe that, but I don't study it. I don't lay awake at night worrying about it. I just think you have to be open to the possibilities."

Fr. William Maestri, former Catholic moral theologian: "Ghosts, spirits of the dead, can't just pop in and out, like on some divine escalator."

The late Edith Layton, Ormond Plantation: "Just because we can't see something does not mean it does not exist. So perhaps ghosts are on a different plane of existence. It would be nice to think that when we go from this body that we've had for our whole life, we go to another plane and that all the knowledge we have amassed is not lost."

The late Archbishop E. J. Johnson, Israelite Divine Black Spiritual Church: "It's all in the mind. If you pray hard enough you can communicate with spirits and there are times you can see them . . . you got earthbound spirits and you got heavenbound spirits. The good spirit will help you and the bad spirit will get you in trouble . . . if you pray and the Holy Ghost takes you, you can talk in Italian, Japanese, or whatever kind of spirit takes you that's what you talk in; they just take control of your body and your voice and they talk in their voice. All this is mystery stuff and a lot of people don't understand it and you can't understand it unless you pray for wisdom and knowledge."

Father Maestri: "There are so many people who are afraid of ghosts and afraid of spirits . . . I don't think it's the dead that we need to be afraid of, I think it's the living. The best thing we can do for the dead is to love them while they're living."

Maida Owens, director of the Louisiana Folklife Program: "I think things are changing concerning beliefs in the supernatural. In the past, ghosts were considered malevolent. They were something to be scared of. But more recently it seems a spirit is less likely to be seen as something that would harm as something that's coming to a friendly visit. I think all of us want to have some kind of assurance about what's going to happen after death. Personally I find it [the possibility of returning spirits] comforting and it doesn't scare me at all . . . during my mother's funeral a friend told me later that the chandeliers suddenly started spinning slightly at one point and it was during the time where one family member was speaking. Then as that person stopped, the chandelier stopped. Now I would like to believe that this is my mother showing approval, letting us know that she liked what she was hearing rather than my mother haunting us or showing disapproval. So I think that's sort of an example of how personal belief systems can determine how we approach these things, whether or not it's a scary ghost or a sweet visit."

Scary or sweet, the haunted label is permanently affixed to *La Belle Dame Créole.*

Former Orleans Criminal Sheriff, Charles Foti: "We have a richer heritage [in New Orleans]. It's like a gumbo. It is like a mixing together of the French and the Spanish and the Italians and the Irish and the African-Americans—everybody together. You make this roux and this gumbo comes out of it and it's rich and it's tasty and it's good and it's earthy, and I think that's what we have that other people don't have."

Father Maestri: "What you have here is all of these influences—cultural, religious, social—and the way they exist in Louisiana is that we take fragments and say, 'Yes, I like that, that fits in here; ooh, I think I like a little of that!' We have become kind of cultural and religious bag ladies. We hate to throw things away. And so instead we claim them as our own, put them in a form we recognize, and it helps us to coexist."

Former director Mary Louise Prudhomme: "You could almost put a fence around Louisiana because it's so different from the rest of the United States. Ghosts, politicians, food, you name it—in those areas we're unique."

Those living in the mystical kingdom of *La Louisiane* are not likely to relinquish their love affair with the past anytime soon. As for this author, I remain enthralled. Ghosts, apparitions, spirits have a very real presence here. It is impossible to sit across from Ruth Bodenheimer in the parlor of the Lanaux Mansion and not be aware of the influence of her in-house decorator, Mr. Charles Andrew Johnson. And it is magical to wander the grounds of Loyd Hall at night, to peer into bedrooms, to stand on the balcony and imagine that maybe, just maybe, I hear the mournful

Harry Henry pulling the bow across the strings of his violin.

I take comfort in the wise counsel of Father Maestri: "We are told by our culture that the only thing that matters is science, which you can taste, see, touch, smell, measure. That's reality. Well, there is something in the human spirit that rebels against that . . . there's whole levels and dimensions of life that are simply going to come out whether we like it or not."

Here in Louisiana we like it very much indeed.

Appendix
Selected Haunted Sites

Plantations

Chretien Point
665 Chretien Point Road
Sunset, LA 70584
337-662-5876

Destrehan Plantation
13034 River Road
Destrehan, LA 70047
985-764-9315

Houmas House
40136 Highway 942
Darrow, LA 70725
225-473-9380

Loyd Hall
292 Loyd Bridge Road
Cheneyville, La 71325
318-776-5641

Madewood Plantation
4250 Highway 308
Napoleonville, LA 70390
504-369-7151

Oak Alley Plantation
3645 Highway 18
Vacherie, LA 70090
225-265-2151

Ormond Plantation
13786 River Road
Destrehan, LA 70047
985-764-8544

Woodland Plantation
21997 Highway 23
West Point a La Hache, LA 70083
800-231-1514

Guest Houses
Lafitte's Guest House
1003 Bourbon Street
New Orleans, LA 70130
504 581-2678

The Lanaux Mansion
547 Esplanade Avenue
New Orleans, LA 70116
504-330-2826

Museums
The Old State Capitol
100 North Boulevard
Baton Rouge, LA
800-488-2968

Restaurants/Music Clubs
New Orleans Creole Cookery
formerly *O'Flaherty's Irish Channel Pub*
508 Toulouse Street
New Orleans, LA 70130
504-524-9632

DVDs
Interviews for many of the chapters were conducted during the filming of the documentaries *The Haunting of Louisiana, Plantation Portraits,* and *Faded Ladies.* For more information or DVDs, contact the author at barbarasillery@gmail.com or www.barbarasillery.com.

(Author photo courtesy of Jeffery D. Meyers)